Efficient Aviation Security

Strengthening the Analytic Foundation for Making Air Transportation Security Decisions

T0289495

Brian A. Jackson, Tom LaTourrette, Edward W. Chan,
Russell Lundberg, Andrew R. Morral, David R. Frelinger

 HOMELAND SECURITY AND DEFENSE CENTER

This monograph results from the RAND Corporation's Investment in People and Ideas program. Support for this program is provided, in part, by donors and by the independent research and development provisions of RAND's contracts for the operation of its U.S. Department of Defense federally funded research and development centers.

Library of Congress Cataloging-in-Publication Data

Jackson, Brian A., 1972-
  Efficient aviation security : strengthening the analytic foundation for making air transportation security decisions / Brian A. Jackson, Tom LaTourrette, Edward W. Chan, Russell Lundberg, Andrew R. Morral, David R. Frelinger.
     pages cm
  Includes bibliographical references.
  ISBN 978-0-8330-7652-6 (pbk. : alk. paper)
  1. Aeronautics—Security measures—United States. I. LaTourrette, Tom, 1963- II. Chan, Edward Wei-Min, 1970- III. Lundberg, Russell. IV. Morral, Andrew R. V. Frelinger, Dave. VI. Title.

  TL725.3.S44J33 2012
  363.28'760973—dc23
                                                                    2012026313

The RAND Corporation is a nonprofit institution that helps improve policy and decisionmaking through research and analysis. RAND's publications do not necessarily reflect the opinions of its research clients and sponsors.
RAND® is a registered trademark.

Cover photo: security screening area at the Denver International Airport (Daniel Paluska).

Published 2012 by the RAND Corporation
1776 Main Street, P.O. Box 2138, Santa Monica, CA 90407-2138
1200 South Hayes Street, Arlington, VA 22202-5050
4570 Fifth Avenue, Suite 600, Pittsburgh, PA 15213-2665
RAND URL: http://www.rand.org/
To order RAND documents or to obtain additional information, contact
Distribution Services: Telephone: (310) 451-7002;
Fax: (310) 451-6915; Email: order@rand.org

Preface

In the decade since the September 11, 2001, terrorist attacks, aviation security has remained a policy area at the forefront of the national policy agenda. Al-Qa'ida has maintained its focus on the U.S. aviation system, and a number of attempted attacks on aircraft have been thwarted in the succeeding years. Internationally, there have been successful attacks on aircraft and airports, and continued adaptation and innovation by terrorist groups has presented aviation planners with a shifting risk environment. The frequent adjustments and systematic tightening of security around the aviation system that have occurred since 9/11 have also put the collateral and intangible effects of security efforts into the national spotlight, with significant controversy about the intrusiveness of security, and stimulated both analysis and debate about whether the benefits of new security measures outweigh their costs.

This document seeks to contribute to the national debate on aviation security by examining a set of issues that are either overlooked or not well captured in analyses of the costs and benefits of security measures. Our effort is motivated by the position that the goal of aviation security is not just to reduce risk in the aviation system, but to do so efficiently—particularly in an era when fiscal constraints require difficult choices between spending resources on security or other important national priorities. We present a series of distinct analyses focused on tools and approaches we believed were missing and therefore hurting efforts to develop efficient security strategies, implement tactics, and get the best outcomes for the resources spent to ensure aviation security.

This monograph results from the RAND Corporation's Investment in People and Ideas program. Support for this program is provided, in part, by donors and by the independent research and development provisions of RAND's contracts for the operation of its U.S. Department of Defense federally funded research and development centers.

The analyses presented here should be of interest to policymakers with responsibility for aviation security design and implementation, analysts and members of the public concerned with security of the national aviation system, and individuals and organizations involved in or dependent on the national air transportation system. Though our focus has been aviation security within the United States, the international nature of the aviation system almost inevitably means that security concerns—and strategies for addressing them—seep across political borders.

This project is the latest in a body of RAND research efforts on homeland security and counterterrorism, with a particular focus on understanding how to assess the cost-effectiveness or efficiency of security and emergency preparedness activities. Other related works include

- Andrew R. Morral and Brian A. Jackson, *Understanding the Role of Deterrence in Counterterrorism Security*, OP-281-RC, 2009
- Jeremy M. Wilson, Brian A. Jackson, Mel Eisman, Paul Steinberg, and K. Jack Riley, *Securing America's Passenger-Rail System*, MG-705-NIJ, 2007
- Brian A. Jackson and David R. Frelinger, *Emerging Threats and Security Planning: How Should We Decide What Hypothetical Threats to Worry About?* OP-256-RC, 2009.

The RAND Homeland Security and Defense Center

This research was conducted within the RAND Homeland Security and Defense Center, which conducts analysis to prepare and protect communities and critical infrastructure from natural disasters and terrorism. Center projects examine a wide range of risk management problems, including coastal and border security, emergency preparedness and response, defense support to civil authorities, transportation security, domestic intelligence, technology acquisition, and related topics. Center clients include the Department of Homeland Security, the Department of Defense, the Department of Justice, and other organizations charged with security and disaster preparedness, response, and recovery. The Homeland Security and Defense Center is a joint center of the RAND National Security Research Division and RAND Infrastructure, Safety, and Environment.

Information about the Homeland Security and Defense Center is available online (http://www.rand.org/multi/homeland-security-and-defense/). Inquiries about homeland security research projects should be sent to:

Andrew Morral, Director
Homeland Security and Defense Center
RAND Corporation
1200 South Hayes Street
Arlington, VA 22202-5050
703-413-1100, x5119
Andrew_Morral@rand.org

Contents

Figures

Tables

Summary

Commercial aviation plays a central role in our daily lives and is an essential part of the national economy. The importance of aviation to both the public and the private sectors drives concerns about how security threats, such as terrorism, could affect the utility, safety, and economic value of those sectors. It is also undeniable that the aviation system has long been an attractive target for terrorists across the political and ideological spectrum. From hijackings in the 1970s to al-Qa'ida in the Arabian Peninsula's disrupted bombing operation in May 2012, terrorists continue to try to exploit the aviation system because of both the visibility and the impact that even semi-successful attacks have produced.

Because of the risk of terrorism to aviation targets, aviation security has grown to become a substantial commercial, political, and social influence in the United States and abroad. The portion of the Transportation Security Administration (TSA) budget in the fiscal year 2011 President's budget devoted to protecting the aviation system was approximately $6.5 billion, counting both the aviation security line item and the budget of the Federal Air Marshal Service (Office of Management and Budget, 2011). Federal expenditures on aviation security represent only a part of the government spending picture, with additional security expenditures made at the state and local levels (e.g., by airport authorities) and by the private sector (e.g., airlines). Security measures also have intangible costs, including the time spent by passengers undergoing security procedures, as well as the hassle and privacy implications of security screening.

Terrorist incidents—most notably 9/11, but also subsequent attempted attacks—have produced significant spikes in policy debate about security performance and effectiveness, and pressure for change has ebbed and flowed as incidents occur and then recede into memory. Reflecting both the dynamics of the policy debate and adaptation by the attackers targeting aviation systems, security technologies and procedures are constantly being developed, tested, implemented, and, occasionally, withdrawn.

Security strategies to protect the aviation system have also been criticized as being reactive and backward-looking, seeming to always be responding to the last observed threat. Concerns have also been raised about the sustainability of security efforts—particularly at passenger checkpoints—that often appear to consist of "ladling on" more and more measures of security in response to every perceived threat.

What the public and other stakeholders expect from security is also complex and has varied over time. At the same time that some constituencies or decisionmakers might express a desire to minimize (or even attempt to eliminate) the risk of terrorist attack on the aviation system, it has also become clear in the past decade that the public's and private-sector organizations' tolerance for inconvenience and other security costs is not inexhaustible. The increasing burden that security places on passengers, cargo shippers, and other businesses, coupled with the perception that some security elements are invasive or unclearly justified, has at times led stakeholders, from passenger associations to the U.S. Congress, to question the decisionmaking process used for pursuing aviation security.

Given the resources and attention devoted to aviation security in an era in which resource constraints are likely to become ever more important in policy decisions, it is important that we approach aviation security in a rational and defensible way. The rationale for security expenditures is to reduce the risk from terrorist threats to the aviation system. If we consider risk to be what we stand to lose from successful attacks, then the benefit of security is the expected consequences of terrorist attacks that are avoided because of the security. To make rational security decisions, the benefits of a measure (or group of measures) must be compared with its varied costs to determine whether those benefits exceed the cost.

In recent years, analysts and researchers both within and outside government have expanded efforts to weigh both the costs and benefits of security interventions. The costs of security are complex, with both immediate, direct components and longer-term, indirect components. Though some costs—such as government expenditures—are comparatively easy to determine, others are less tangible and quantifiable. Substantial progress has been made, but we are still far from the point where policy and security analysis can fully support building efficient and sustainable aviation security strategies.

Even more poorly understood are the benefits of aviation security efforts. Because the magnitude of the risk to the commercial aviation system is low and poorly characterized, it is difficult to assess the extent to which this risk may be decreased after the introduction of a particular security investment. And, even if we determine that the risk has decreased, it is hard to know whether or how much it decreased because of some deliberate action we have taken or because of some other factors whose effect we do not appreciate.

More complete understanding of the costs and benefits of security measures is needed. Only with clear understanding of what security measures truly cost and what we get when we buy those measures will it be possible to get closer to the efficient security we must aspire to in a world of finite resources and many varied policy areas that demand funding and attention.

Addressing Key Uncertainties and Knowledge Gaps in Aviation Security

The goal of crafting truly efficient aviation security strategies is hampered by a variety of uncertainties. It will always be difficult to draw clear, quantitative conclusions about terrorist preferences (threat) and security performance (vulnerability) given the evolution and adaptation by both attackers and defenders. Historical data are one window, but past performance—on both sides of the conflict—provides only some insight into likely future results. Meeting analysts and policy-makers' eternal pleas for more and better intelligence information could help reduce this uncertainty, but the ability of attackers to change their behavior means that some uncertainty will always remain. Other uncertainties affect the ability to perform detailed cost-benefit type studies, including quantification of the full costs of attempted or successful attacks on aviation targets, most notably their indirect costs; the full costs of security measures; and their full effects both on the ability of attackers to successfully stage attacks and their decisions to do so in the first place. These too are areas where "more and better analysis" could reduce the levels of uncertainty, but only to a point—as changes in society, public preferences, and the nature of terrorist adversaries will make any estimates perishable at best.

However, in spite of uncertainty, it is still possible to perform analyses that define key tradeoffs, map out the major sources of uncertainty, and make it possible to make more informed security decisions. In the work described here, we address several of these areas of uncertainty and analytical complexity:

- Predicting future terrorist risks with certainty will never be possible. However, retrospective analysis of historical threats coupled with systematic approaches for projecting how those threats could change going forward can help to identify security strategies that are relevant across known and possible attack methods—limiting the sensitivity of security performance to future attacker behavior.
- While it is broadly accepted that security measures have intangible costs—and that those costs affect the utility of the aviation system—it is less clear how to appropriately capture them in security analysis. Building out from accepted cost-benefit methodologies, we demonstrate how even approximate estimates for such effects can be used when different security measures are compared or—as has been the strategy in aviation—when increasing numbers of security measures are added on top of one another as threats change over time.
- Though the security strategy of combining many types of security measures into a "layered defense" has been accepted doctrine

for many years, many analyses of that strategy have not fully explored how different layers interact with one another to deliver a net protective posture for the aviation system. In other contexts, assessing the benefits of combining multiple interventions has not always been straightforward—and multiple measures together can produce outcomes that are less than the sum of the individual measures alone. Translating the lessons from these other fields (notably safety engineering) provides approaches to address such concerns in assessments of layered security measures.

- In considering the effect of security measures on terrorism risk, one area that has posed problems has been the effect of deterrence— or the way the presence of security shapes the choices made by attackers before or during an attack. Though it is generally accepted that deterrence is a significant driver of the benefits for some security measures, understanding how to address it in cost-benefit analyses has been less clear. Adapting techniques of break-even analysis can provide a way to do so: Assessments of individual security measures should include the calculation of how much risk reduction (including via deterrence) a given security measure must provide in order to be cost-effective.

- Another area where our analysis reveals useful insights for security decisionmaking is understanding the merits of preferential screening proposals, such as a trusted traveler program. Despite interest in pursuing such a program, progress has been stymied because the potential benefit depends on behaviors of passengers and terrorists that are highly uncertain. Our analysis shows that even when uncertainties are great we can identify plausible conditions under which a trusted traveler program would reduce risk. Two key factors are the fraction of the traveling public that enrolls in the trusted traveler program and the fraction of terrorists that do so. Though decisionmakers cannot control these factors, they can influence them. Such insights add some clarity to a debate beset with uncertainty and ambivalence.

- Finally, a more general area in which our analysis provides helpful insight in addressing uncertainties is in the use of modeling to understand terrorism risks. The limited amount and quality of data on aviation terrorism incidents combined with our poor understanding of terrorist behavior makes predictive modeling of terrorism risk untenable. The uncertainties associated with any effort to identify best estimates of risk or risk reduction are so great as to make the result meaningless. However, models can be designed and used for less precise and final purposes. Rather than attempting to account for all potential influences and the complex relationships among them, a simpler, low-resolution model may have just a few key parameters and allow users to develop plausible hypotheses about the conditions under which security systems might produce benefits.

Looking to the Future

In the majority of the analyses discussed in this document, we considered the benefit of security measures and examined various types of uncertainties that can affect how those benefits are measured and valued. The four studies that looked at the benefits of security (discussed in Chapters Four through Seven) each capture different complexities regarding human adaptive behavior. Though adaptation by terrorist attackers is frequently the focus in security planning, our examination of a potential trusted traveler program highlights that decisions made by passengers can have their own security implications. Irrespective of the source of the challenge, when considering a potential security investment or evaluating one that is in place now, we do not want to overstate the expected benefits, which can happen if we either neglect interactions between measures in a multilayered security system or ignore how attackers could try to use the characteristics of our security strategies to their benefit.

Looking to the future of aviation security in the United States, the resource constraints that are almost certain to affect most policy areas will be a challenge. For organizations and people charged with protecting citizens from harm, the potential for cuts in resources is always difficult to consider and to implement, and there will always be an understandable trepidation to make cuts out of fear that imprudent action will undermine effective security efforts. The politics surrounding security is a challenge as well. Since criticizing security performance is a staple of partisan political debate after even unsuccessful terrorist attacks, there is a potent disincentive to scale back security in any form. But if a sufficient analytical basis for assessing security measures and strategies is available, these trepidations might be reduced and resource constraints converted from a crisis into an opportunity. Constraints force choices, which in turn force evaluation to help ensure that we are not spending limited national resources in ways that are not achieving what they are intended to achieve. In aviation security, where the total cost of the national effort has expanded significantly since 9/11, such an evaluation could pay dividends not just in reduced national expenditures, but also by helping to identify ways to get better security for less cost—more efficient aviation security—that could make our homeland security efforts more sustainable and make the country better off in the long run.

Acknowledgments

In the course of this study, many people made substantial contributions that were instrumental to the success of the effort. We would like to acknowledge Robert Poole of the Reason Foundation and Sheldon H. Jacobson of the University of Illinois for their contributions. We would also like to acknowledge the representatives of a major U.S. airline who kindly provided us with information that contributed to our analysis of trusted traveler programs. Though we are unable to identify the individuals or the airline by name, that we cannot do so does not lessen our gratitude for their assistance.

During the course of the project, we presented preliminary results of the analysis to a variety of individuals both inside and outside government who provided input and suggestions. Outstanding among these is Andrew Cox of the Transportation Security Administration.

Within RAND, we would acknowledge the suggestions and contributions to the study and its varied products from Jack Riley, Jim Chiesa, Debra Knopman, Henry Willis, and Eric Peltz. In addition, a number of RAND colleagues participated in the project in its early phases or in related studies whose contributions are gratefully acknowledged. They included Mel Eisman, Zev Winkelman, Henry Willis, James Anderson, Paul Dreyer, Kay Sullivan Faith, Julie Kim, and Paul Steinberg.

Scott Savitz of RAND and Sheldon H. Jacobson of the University of Illinois provided detailed and valuable reviews of the document. All shortcomings remain the sole responsibility of the authors.

Abbreviations

DHS	U.S. Department of Homeland Security
FAA	Federal Aviation Administration
FAM	Federal Air Marshal
GAO	U.S. Government Accountability Office or, prior to 2004, U.S. General Accounting Office
IG	Inspector General
LTTE	Liberation Tigers of Tamil Eelam
MANPAD	man-portable antiaircraft missile
RITA	Research and Innovative Technology Administration
TSA	Transportation Security Administration

CHAPTER ONE

Introduction: The Goal of Efficient Security

Tom LaTourrette and Brian A. Jackson

Aviation plays a central role in our daily lives and is an essential part of the national economy. In 2010, over 8.7 million commercial flights transported more than 629 million passengers more than 554 billion revenue-passenger miles domestically (RITA, 2011b).[1] An additional 1.3 million international flights transported approximately 158 million passengers to and from the United States (RITA, 2011a). There are also several times as many personal and corporate flights each year as there are commercial ones.[2] In addition, in 2010, U.S. carriers shipped 23 million revenue-tons of air cargo domestically and internationally (RITA, 2011a). Aviation makes a substantial contribution to the economy: U.S. air carriers' operating revenues totaled approximately $175 billion in 2010 (RITA, 2011a), and more inclusive estimates put the annual contribution of aviation to the U.S. economy in the trillions of dollars.[3] The importance of aviation to both the public and the private sectors drives concerns about how security threats, such as terrorism, could affect the utility, safety, and economic value of the aviation system.

It is also undeniable that the aviation system has long been an attractive target for terrorists across the political and ideological spec-

---

[1] "Revenue-passenger miles" is the product of paying passengers on a flight multiplied by the miles traveled by the flight.

[2] According to Federal Aviation Administration (FAA) estimates, in 2009 (the latest year available at the time of this writing), there were more than 35 million landings by general aviation and air taxi aircraft nationwide (FAA, 2012).

[3] A 2006 FAA put the value at approximately $1.2 trillion (FAA, 2008).

trum. From hijackings in the 1970s to al-Qa'ida in the Arabian Peninsula's disrupted bombing operation in May 2012, terrorists continue to try to exploit the aviation system because of both the visibility and the impact that even semi-successful attacks have produced. As Transportation Security Administration (TSA) director John Pistole noted in a recent interview (Fallows and Goldberg, 2010),

> There's a fascination, I think, with blowing planes—especially passenger planes—out of the air. There is a psychological trauma that the terrorists see. That's their gold standard.

Overshadowing the decades-long history of aviation terrorism are the September 11, 2001, attacks, in which the aviation system was used to perpetrate the most consequential attacks in the history of modern terrorism.

Because of the risk of terrorism to aviation targets, aviation security has grown to become a substantial commercial, political, and social influence in the United States and abroad. Prior to 9/11, aviation security was implemented through a regulatory model, with the FAA playing the central federal role. Since 9/11 and the subsequent governmental reorganization, the central federal actor is the TSA, through which the federal government has directly implemented many aviation security measures and initiatives.[4] The portion of the TSA budget in the fiscal year 2011 President's budget devoted to protecting the aviation system was approximately $6.5 billion, counting both the aviation security line item and the budget of the Federal Air Marshal Service (Office of Management and Budget, 2011). Federal expenditures on aviation security represent only a part of the government spending picture, with additional security expenditures made at the state and local levels (e.g., by airport authorities) and by the private sector (e.g., airlines). Private projections of the aviation security market worldwide currently fall in the tens of billions of dollars annually.[5] Security mea-

---

[4]   A number of reviews of the history of aviation security are available in the literature, including Seidenstat, 2004; Schroer, 2004; Krause, 2003; and Thomas, 2008.

[5]   See, for example, Visiongain, 2011.

sures have intangible costs as well, including the time spent and hassle endured by passengers undergoing security procedures, as well as the privacy implications of security screening. The wait times in security lines at airports are also unpredictable: Waits are relatively short under most conditions but sometimes reach tens of minutes.[6] An aviation industry estimate of the costs borne by airlines and passengers (including a value for time spent in security delays) was $7.4 billion annually (International Air Transport Association [IATA], 2011).

Terrorist incidents—most notably 9/11, but also subsequent attempted attacks—have produced significant spikes in policy debate about security performance and effectiveness, and pressure for change has ebbed and flowed as incidents occur and then recede into memory. Reflecting both the dynamics of the policy debate and adaptation by the attackers targeting aviation systems, security technologies and procedures are constantly being developed, tested, implemented, and, occasionally, withdrawn. Since 2001, new measures have included restrictions on liquids in carry-ons in response to liquid explosive threats, new imaging devices (including both x-ray and millimeter wave technologies) to see under clothing, and use of physical swabs and analytic devices to detect explosive residues on passengers' hands. Security technologies that have been tested and withdrawn include so-called "puffer portals" that sought to detect explosive residues on clothing by dislodging them with a blast of air.

Security strategies to protect the aviation system during this period have also been criticized as being reactive and backward-looking, seeming to always be responding to the last observed threat. Concerns have also been raised about the sustainability of security efforts—particularly at passenger checkpoints—that often appear to consist of "ladling on" more and more measures of security in response to every perceived threat.

What the public and other stakeholders expect from security is also complex and has varied over time. At the same time that some

---

[6] The TSA previously published wait time data on its website, but the practice has been discontinued. Some—now-out-of-date—data are available on other Internet websites that republished the data at the time.

constituencies or decisionmakers might express a desire to minimize (or even attempt to eliminate) the risk of terrorist attack on the aviation system, it has also become clear in the past decade that the public's and private-sector organizations' tolerance for inconvenience and other security costs is not inexhaustible. The increasing burden that security places on passengers, cargo shippers, and other businesses, coupled with the perception that some security elements are invasive or unclearly justified, has at times led people and institutions from passengers to the U.S. Congress to question the decisionmaking process used for pursuing aviation security.

Significant analytic and policy attention has been devoted to the topic of aviation security, especially since 9/11. Researchers in fields ranging from political science and economics to sociology and psychology have examined many aspects of aviation security practices and the interactions of people and institutions in the aviation security system. Analyses by the U.S. Department of Homeland Security (DHS) Inspector General (IG), the U.S. Government Accountability Office (GAO), the Congressional Research Service, the National Academy of Sciences, and investigative reporters have examined individual security practices, technologies, and the aviation security enterprise as a whole, with a focus on examining the costs and benefits of aviation security and the development of rational, transparent methodologies for aviation security decisionmaking.[7]

---

[7]   The breadth of the literature on aviation security in academic and policy discussion makes it difficult to capture it in a complete form. Key, exemplary, and recent sources discussing both overall aviation security strategies and measures include Bragdon, 2008; Johnstone, 2006; White House Commission on Aviation Safety and Security, 1997; Wilkinson and Jenkins, 1999; Kaufmann, 2010; Poole, 2006; National Research Council, Committee on Commercial Aviation Security, 1996; National Research Council, Panel on Assessment of Technologies Deployed to Improve Aviation Security, 1999; Jenkins, 1989; DHS IG, 2009, 2010; GAO, 2005, 2007a, 2008a, 2008b, 2009b, 2009c, 2010, 2011; Elias, 2009, 2010a, 2010b; Butcher, 2011; U.S. House of Representatives, 2008, 2009a, 2009b, 2009c 2010a, 2010b; U.S. Senate, 2010.

Not Just More Security, But More *Efficient* Security

Given the resources and attention devoted to aviation security and the inconvenience and costs it causes to passengers, airports, and airlines, it is important that we approach aviation security in a rational and defensible way. The rationale for security expenditures is to reduce the risk from terrorist threats to the aviation system. If we consider risk to be what we stand to lose from successful attacks, then the benefit of security is the expected consequences of terrorist attacks that are avoided or whose consequences are lessened because of the security. To make rational security decisions, the benefit of a measure (or group of measures) must be compared with its varied costs to determine whether those benefits exceed the cost. In the parlance of cost-benefit analysis, this is a condition in which the *net benefit*, or benefit minus cost, is positive. Beyond simply *having* any positive net benefit, the size of that benefit compared with the cost of the measure is important as well. For example, though spending $100 million to obtain $101 million in benefits would be technically justifiable, a security measure that cost $10 million and achieved $11 million in benefits would be preferable from a policy perspective. The absolute net benefit ($1 million) is the same in both cases, but the $10 million option is more cost-effective. Particularly in an era in which budgets are expected to be under significant pressure, simply getting a benefit from security should not be enough: We should endeavor to get the most security for the least cost—efficient security.[8] We should also remember that any funds devoted to security come at the expense of other government or private-sector priorities, and we should be cognizant that there might be opportunities to achieve greater reductions in risk in areas outside aviation.

In recent years, analysts and researchers both within and outside government have expanded efforts to weigh both the costs and

---

[8] Some analysts have argued against the use of the language of efficiency with respect to security efforts, though the objection is based on the argument that a focus on efficiency risks greater attention being paid to such measures as throughput of security processes and less to the *quality* of the security provided (see Johnston, 2004). We are not arguing for that here, rather that we need to focus on efficiency as "quality per cost."

benefits of security interventions. The costs of security are complex, with both immediate, direct components and longer-term, indirect components. Though some—such as government expenditures—are comparatively easy to determine, others are less tangible and quantifiable. Understanding the benefits of security is similarly complicated by both the uncertainty in the extent to which security reduces the frequency of successful attacks and the difficulties in estimating the value of avoided losses, such as fatalities, injuries, property damage, and such indirect effects as changes in economic activity resulting from the perception of reduced terrorist risk.

Advances have been made in developing analytical techniques and approaches on both sides of the counterterrorism "balance sheet"— both in general and for aviation security in particular. The breadth of this growing literature resists terse summary. However, to provide a context for subsequent discussion, we will briefly sketch its contours:

- In response to concern about terrorist attackers changing their behaviors—and how those changes affect the performance of security measures—there has been significant work to understand how to address such uncertainty and variability in benefits assessment. Studies have included work to characterize attacker adaptation behavior in detail (Jackson et al., 2005a, 2005b, 2007; Cragin and Daly, 2004; Davis and Cragin, 2009; McCormick, 2003)[9] and risk modeling approaches to use different types of information on adversary preferences to integrate adaptation into values used for assessing security performance (e.g., Bier et al., 2008; Bier, 2005; Cox, Jr., 2009; Ezell et al., 2010; Keeney and von Winterfeldt, 2010; Keeney, 2007; Parnell, Smith, and Moxley, 2010). Approaching the problem from a different direction, analysts have also developed more approximate methods that simply accept the uncertainty associated with adversary behavior and assess security measures against a range of risk levels—thereby bracketing "how good the measure would have to be" to be valu-

---

[9]   While this issue has received significant recent focus, it was a concern long before 9/11 (e.g., Cauley and Im, 1988).

able for different levels of risk (e.g., Willis and LaTourrette, 2008; Jackson, 2009a; Stewart, 2010; Akhtar, Bjørnskau, and Veisten, 2010; Stewart and Mueller, 2011).

- Other analytical efforts have focused on better methods to design and implement individual classes of security measures or to weigh their balance of benefits and costs. For example, there is a deep literature drawing on operations research focused on screening processes for baggage and passengers (e.g., Leone and Liu, 2005; Jacobson et al., 2003; Feng, 2007; Barnett et al., 2001) and multiple studies regarding the protection of aircraft from man-portable missiles (Chow et al., 2005; von Winterfeldt and O'Sullivan, 2006). For some security measures, assessment efforts have in some cases been more qualitative but in other cases taken on the underlying basis for security efforts and asked more fundamental questions about their utility or the key variables affecting their performance (e.g., Holmes, 2009, 2011; Kaufman and Carlson, 2010; National Academies, 2008; Ghylin, Drury, and Schwaninger, 2006; von Bastian, Schwaninger, and Michel, 2008; Drury, Ghylin, and Holness, 2006).

- Because of both concerns about the burden of security on travelers and the view that intensively screening individuals who are unlikely to be terrorists is inefficient, there have been studies of how screening might be done selectively. Negative profiling, or identifying portions of the population who are viewed as more likely to be threats and screening them more intensively than the general public, is one strategy. Extensive work has been done on such profiling, highlighting a number of problems, including the high number of innocent people likely to fall into any profile (Martonosi and Barnett, 2006; McLay, Lee, and Jacobson, 2010; Cavusoglu, Koh, and Raghunathan, 2010; Press, 2010; Persico and Todd, 2005) and the opportunity for attackers to recruit members who fall outside the profile conditions (Jackson et al., 2007; Chakrabarti and Strauss, 2002). Other analyses have examined positive profiling (trusted or registered traveler programs) as alternative strategies (see GAO, 2002a; Jackson, Chan, and LaTourrette, 2012).

- In addition to efforts focused at the level of individual security measures, there has also been considerable analytic effort aimed at developing methods to assess security efforts—for aviation, other potential targets, and the nation overall—or for specified portfolios of security measures (e.g., Belcore and Ellig, 2008; Stewart and Mueller, 2008; Lord et al., 2010; Akhtar, Bjørnskau, and Veisten, 2010; Pacheco et al., 2011; Wilson et al., 2007). Such analyses have included the development of methods to address how different security measures can move risk around a transportation system and the various tradeoffs among different approaches to protect a target from varied types of attack.

Although substantial progress has been made, we are still far from the point where policy and security analysis can fully support building efficient and sustainable aviation security strategies and developing tactical implementations of such strategies. More complete understanding of the costs and benefits of security measures is needed. A particular difficulty is understanding the costs associated with the effects of security on system functionality. On the benefit side of the ledger, better understanding of how to analyze security "as a system" is central, given the complexity of the task of protecting any highly distributed critical infrastructure system. Only with clear understandings of what security measures truly cost and what we get when we buy those measures will it be possible to get closer to the efficient security we must aspire to in a world of finite resources and many varied policy areas that demand funding and attention.

About This Report

This report presents a set of distinct analyses that contribute to filling some of the current gaps in analysis of the costs, benefits, and efficiency of aviation security measures and strategies. Chapter Two discusses terrorist risk to the aviation system, considering both historical and prospective future threats. Chapter Three examines uncertainty in the costs of security measures and approximate ways to address that uncertainty in policy analysis. Chapter Four focuses on layered security strategies and the assessment of performance of different security measures used in concert. Chapter Five examines the issue of deterrence, an important effect of security that is often neglected in cost-benefit or cost-effectiveness analysis. Chapter Six looks at how intended and unintended consequences of security measures trade off and affect outcomes, focusing on the specific issue of a trusted traveler program to focus security screening activities. Chapter Seven looks at assessment as a system, exploring both the modeling challenges related to benefits estimation and integrative approaches for making security policy choices. Finally, Chapter Eight provides a set of conclusions derived from the preceding chapters.

CHAPTER TWO

The Problem to Be Solved: Aviation Terrorism Risk Past, Present, and Future

Brian A. Jackson and David R. Frelinger

The goal of aviation security is to address threats posed to targets in the air transportation system. The basis of a rational and effective security strategy must therefore be a picture of the security threats that need to be addressed, paired with information on their seriousness to help set priorities and to assess the value of different security strategies. In homeland security policymaking, the use of risk analysis has become a central element of decisionmaking and the preferred approach for informing priority setting and evaluation efforts. In principle, risk provides a common basis for comparison among the outcomes of a wide variety of terrorist attacks, natural phenomena, accidents, and other damaging events. The core components of risk are the probability that a damaging event will occur and the consequences of it occurring. The product of those two values can be used to compare, for example, the risks of more common, less damaging incidents with much rarer but more consequential ones. Though risk does provide a "common denominator" and important input for such comparisons, it cannot be the sole basis for decisionmaking—given issues such as different levels of uncertainty in estimates of different hazard types and the vastly different time periods required for risk-reducing investments to pay off for common versus very low-probability risks—meaning that such decisions are better viewed as risk-*informed* rather than risk-*determined*.

When assessing risk from terrorism, the two components of risk are generally broken down further, into three elements—threat, vulnerability, and consequences—to reflect that risk of a particular type of terrorist attack is shaped by the choices made by attackers and the nature of targets and defenses (Willis et al., 2005). Though it is intuitive that terrorist risk is a function of adversary intent and capability (threat, or probability of an attack being attempted), target characteristics (vulnerability, the probability of damage of an attempted attack), and the scale of the potential damage inflicted by successful attacks (consequences), characterizing risks and strategies for managing risks in terms of these components, particularly into the future, is problematic. For example, threat is affected by attacker assumptions about vulnerability, and any steps taken to reduce vulnerability or consequences from specific attacks will create incentives for attackers to change the types of attacks they attempt. Simple assessments of threat, vulnerability, and consequences in isolation ignore these interactions and correlations (Cox, Jr., 2008).[1] Nevertheless, the three components are still generally viewed as a useful framework for examining the different drivers of terrorist risk for analytic purposes.

A clear example of this dynamic is the way security implemented since 9/11 has caused the terrorist threat to shift from hijackings to bombings and other types of attacks. This shaping of terrorist intent and attack behavior by defensive measures is not a new phenomenon. Interest in aviation attacks has been an enduring part of the terrorist landscape, and security designed to prevent such attacks is not new either. The need to address politically motivated terrorist attacks on aviation, notably hijackings, was the driving force for the creation of what has become the modern aviation security system. The steps taken to make hijackings more difficult led terrorists to choose other strategies, including bombings of planes while airborne.

The complex nature of aviation security threats—and the coevolution of those threats with the security measures designed to address them—makes developing a useful projection of future risk particu-

---

[1]   While this creates well-documented problems that are the focus of ongoing research in the risk analysis community (see, for example, Bier, 2005; National Research Council, Committee on Methodological Improvements to the Department of Homeland Security's Biological Agent Risk Analysis, 2008b; Cox, Jr., 2008, 2009; Dillon, Liebe, and Bestafka, 2009; Parnell, Smith, and Moxley, 2010; Brown and Cox, Jr., 2011), use of these three categories is still a useful structure for considering different drivers of terrorism risk in analyses.

larly challenging.[2] The significant changes that have been made to the aviation system over time mean that simple extrapolation from past to future threats produces a misleading picture. At the same time, there are problems inherent in focusing only on recent threats, or only on projections of what future terrorists might attempt, since doing so could bias our understanding and could even provide our adversaries with opportunities to manipulate our behavior to their advantage. In the remainder of this chapter, we navigate these two issues—examining historical risks and discussing what they can (and cannot) teach us, and exploring ways to think rationally about possible future threats—and then conclude by building a more general and qualitative approach to combine both types of information to provide a foundation for examining security strategies.

Learning from the Past: Historical Terrorist Attacks on Aviation

Though our domestic focus has been on al-Qa'ida and its attempted attacks onboard aircraft, threats to air transportation systems are in fact more diverse.[3] Over the course of aviation history, terrorist attacks have varied significantly in complexity and have been staged by actors whose motives have varied across a wide spectrum. While al-Qa'ida's attempts to bomb planes have been high-profile components of the contemporary threat, types of attacks that might be considered relics of the past still occur today. Hijackings of aircraft by individuals simply seeking transport from one country to another, a prominent feature

---

[2]   For example, see Jackson et al., 2007a; Jackson, 2009b; Kenney, 2006; Jackson et al., 2005b.

[3]   Though our focus is on terrorism, actions by individual criminals have brought down flights, and the aviation system is used as a route for smuggling and other criminal activity. Some criminal threats are similar enough to terrorism that protective measures to address terrorist threats may also address the criminal ones as well—producing an additional benefit stream for the investment necessary to put those measures in place.

in the early history of skyjacking and air terrorism, still occur.[4] Furthermore, the terrorist threat to aviation is similarly more diverse than the string of recent domestic attempts might suggest. Given this wide variety, the starting point for an assessment of risk must be an understanding of the ways that attackers could attack the aviation system to cause damage and disruption—and what types of consequences different attack options can produce. In this section, we explore historical attacks—using them as a window into different ways that aviation could be attacked and the basis for a framework for thinking through risks—and then look at both the opportunities and challenges for applying historical data in analysis of terrorist risk to aviation.

Describing Past Terrorist Attacks on Aviation Targets

As a way to begin to map out that threat landscape, examples of historical attacks on the aviation system can provide an initial set of signposts to frame the range of possible attack options.

- *Attacks against different components of the system.* Historically, attackers have focused more on attacking airplanes than airports or other infrastructure that supports aviation. Hijackings to gain control of airplanes (whether for transport or to hold the plane and passengers at risk in an effort achieve other goals or coerce governments to accede to various attacker demands) were very prominent early in the history of aviation terrorism, though attacks to directly damage planes also represented an important part of the threat. Emblematic examples of attacks on airplanes include the bombing of Pan Am Flight 103 over Lockerbie, Scotland, in 1988 and the many hijackings of airliners by individuals seeking transport to Cuba in the 1970s. Though less prominent, attackers also staged many attacks on airports. Operations have included standoff attacks (e.g., rockets and mortars) in which weapons were launched into airports; armed assaults, such as the

---

[4]   For example, in 2003, two hijackings occurred of Cuban aircraft by individuals seeking to travel to the United States (Aviation Safety Network, 2012a, records 20030331-0 and 20030319-0).

Japanese Red Army's attack on Lod Airport in Israel in 1972; and emplaced bombs in publicly accessible areas.[5]

- *Attacks with very different goals.* Examining terrorist operations demonstrates that attackers' goals can vary. The contrast between "traditional hijackings," in which aircraft and their passengers were seized to set up mobile hostage situations to attract attention for extended periods, and the hijackings involved in the 9/11 attacks is an extreme example. Some terrorist attacks on the aviation infrastructure have been designed to produce disruption rather than destruction (e.g., incidents involving the planting of "dummy" explosive devices that could not go off but still require responses that disrupt airport operations). Looking beyond terrorism, individuals have carried out aviation attacks not for political or religious purposes but to commit suicide—and choosing to do so in a way that resulted in the loss of the entire aircraft and the death of many other individuals.[6]
- *Attacks using varied weapons and tactics.* Aviation attacks have drawn on the full range of weapons and tactics available to modern terrorist groups. Some operations have been relatively simple, such as planting bombs or using standoff weapons (e.g., the Provisional Irish Republican Army's attack on Heathrow Airport using timed mortars in 1994). More elaborate operations and tactics have been used as well, including the previously mentioned Lod Airport armed assault and an attack by the Liberation Tigers of Tamil Eelam (LTTE) on the Bandaranaike Airport Sri Lanka in 2001. That attack, which involved a multiperson suicide squad penetrating the airport, resulted in damage to a number of

---

[5]   Terrorist groups have also staged many attacks on airline offices. The rationale for such attacks was often the group's linkage of particular airlines to specific nations (e.g., of Aeroflot with the Soviet Union or El Al with Israel). Though such operations still occur and offices represent comparatively soft targets for attack, since they are not part of the aviation transportation system relevant to this study—i.e., the part of that system covered by aviation security measures—we have excluded such operations from our analysis. Attacks on specific individuals associated with airlines (e.g., assassination of a regional manager of an airline by a terrorist group) are similarly excluded.

[6]   See Aviation Safety Network, 2012b.

military and civilian aircraft. In a subsequent attack targeting a military airfield, the LTTE actually fielded an "air force" of light planes and dropped bombs on planes from above.

- *Attacks via different attack vectors.* Even for operations with common targets, attackers have used different approaches to stage the attacks. Looking only at attacks with the goal of aerial detonation of an explosive device inside an airplane, attackers have tried, sometimes successfully, to get weapons onto planes through a variety of paths or attack vectors. The flying public is most familiar with attack vectors where terrorists enter as passengers, seeking to bring weapons onto aircraft. However, groups have attempted to infiltrate explosives onto planes through a range of other strategies, including hiding them in luggage (e.g., Pan Am Flight 103), infiltrating the cargo system (e.g., al-Qa'ida in the Arabian Peninsula's 2010 attack attempts), using an insider with access to planes (e.g., in 1986, the LTTE coerced a customs official into planting a bomb for the group by threatening his family with harm), and smuggling ingredients for a device through security to be assembled later (e.g., the liquid explosives plot in 2006).

Such a walk through individual examples of past attacks emphasizes how the characteristics of terrorist attacks on the aviation system can vary across the threat spectrum. To be useful, a risk assessment requires a framework that can capture the variety but still support analysis at a level of detail that is understandable and useful. Using historical attacks as a jumping-off point for developing a framework, we focused on the first two of the bullets above: the components of the air transportation system under attack and the central goals of those attacks. In the first category, we defined three main classes of targets that can be readily aligned with available data on historical operations:

- airplanes (both on the ground and in flight)
- airports (which we use as a general term for the immediate ground infrastructure supporting air operations, including central cargo facilities and passenger airports)

part to economic conditions unconnected with the attack (Ito and Lee, 2005).

- A RAND analysis supporting assessment of the installation of defenses against man-portable antiaircraft missiles (MANPADs) on commercial aircraft estimated the direct costs of a single attack at $1 billion, when a monetized number for the value of lives lost in the aircraft were included.[12] Indirect costs were estimated as potentially much higher but were expected to be driven by the policy response to an attack (i.e., an air system shutdown) rather than the attack itself. They were estimated as likely to reach $15 billion based on estimates of the economic effects of the air system shutdowns put in place after the 9/11 attacks (Chow et al., 2005).

- Economic cost estimates for earlier air terrorism incidents have been much lower, however. For example, when Pan Am Flight 103 was downed over Lockerbie, Scotland, in 1988 by a cargo bomb, killing several hundred people (including 11 on the ground), reported values for insured losses were in the low hundreds of millions in 2001 dollars (Swiss Re values quoted in Saxton, 2002). Similarly, in time-series analyses of the effect of terrorism on aviation (most post-9/11), the effect of the Lockerbie attack—which is not even mentioned by name among a number of other shocks— is assessed as comparatively modest and transitory (Ito and Lee, 2005). This finding is echoed by other analyses that observed no "fear effect" on behavior from previous terrorist incidents (Peter-

---

[12] Looking at the economic costs associated with individual deaths in accidents or terrorist attacks, while a difficult topic, is a necessary part of understanding their full economic impacts. Analyses of per-person litigated compensation paid after aviation accidents from 1970 to 1984 found an average total cost of $412,000 per person (1986 dollars, including all legal expenditures), or approximately $800,000 in 2009 dollars (Kakalik et al., 1988)— although companion research demonstrated that compensation represented only a fraction of the total economic losses associated with individuals' loss of life by approximately a factor of four on average (King and Smith, 1988). Other studies—for both accident analysis and regulatory purposes—have also sought to assign economic values to human lives, producing a range of values that are either explicitly or implicitly applied (reviewed in Willis and LaTourrette, 2008). These studies tend to find much higher values, typically in the range of $5 million to $8 million, for the economic value of a life lost.

son et al., 2007). Even if the economic consequence values for the Lockerbie attack were multiplied five- or even tenfold to account for uninsured and other costs unaccounted for, the result would be in the low billions of dollars rather than tens of billions.

- Stepping away from aviation disasters caused by terrorism, there is also a (somewhat dated) literature examining the economic costs of aviation accidents and disasters. These analyses have produced mixed results. Some analyses of major crashes showed, for example, no abnormal negative returns in the stock prices of airlines affected by large crashes between 1965 and 1984 (Davidson III, Chandy, and Cross, 1987). Contrasting with examinations of the 9/11 attacks, some earlier analyses also found little effect on the demand for airline travel from accidents (Borenstein and Zimmerman, 1988). Borenstein and Zimmerman did observe significant effects on airline firm stock prices as a result of accidents. Others find evidence of passengers switching from an airline affected by a crash to others, and some general demand reduction after an incident (Bosch, Eckard, and Singal, 1998). However, even in studies that observe effects of significant accidents on firms or aviation in general, the scales of those effects are modest when compared with the high-end estimates for the effects of 9/11.

To support analysis, the disparate estimates must be reconciled—at least to some extent—to provide consequence ranges to compare with the costs of security or other policy interventions. Direct costs from single incidents involving loss of an aircraft clearly fall into the range of the low billions of dollars (including loss of the airframe and some economic measure for passenger loss of life). Whether the economic consequences of attacks exceed those levels depends nearly entirely on the assumed scale of indirect effects associated with the attack. For example, major drivers of estimated consequences in some recent analyses have included whether an attack would result in aviation system shutdown (e.g., Chow et al., 2005) and expected effects on air transport.

It is clear that aviation attacks can produce very substantial economic consequences, but also that those incidents are clearly outliers.

Even when caused by terrorist attack, incidents involving the loss of an airframe are much more likely to produce costs in the range of the low billions of dollars—with the escalation potential of those costs driven by the response to the attack (i.e., whether air traffic is shut down and for how long) rather than the attack itself. Attacks that do not result in loss of an airframe, which represent the vast majority of terrorist attacks on aviation, produce consequences in the millions rather than billions of dollars. Because of their rarity, history provides little basis for assessing the monetary consequences of attacks specifically targeting aviation infrastructure.

Limits to Using Historical Data for Characterizing Terrorist Risk to Aviation

A traditional risk analysis approach to assessing aviation terrorism requires assessing threat (the probability that different types of attacks are attempted), vulnerability (the probability that they would succeed in causing damage if attempted), and the consequences of the different attack types. Historical experience with terrorism targeted at aviation provides information to inform parts of such a risk analysis, but using *only* historical data has the potential to bias results in ways that are potentially problematic.

The most straightforward element of risk analysis that can be most directly built on a foundation of historical data is assessment of the **consequences** of attacks. Consequences—whether human casualties or financial costs—are driven by the nature of the targets involved (how many people are on planes, what the planes cost) and the physical properties of the weapons used to stage attacks. Past attacks can therefore provide a basis for making estimates of the outcomes of attacks in which attackers gain control of an aircraft and can use it to strike other targets (e.g., 9/11), destroy an aircraft in flight, take hostages, or stage more modest-scale attacks on aircraft or ground portions of the system. For these types of attacks, human and monetary consequences are linked, with policy responses potentially magnifying the latter. Attacks on infrastructure decouple financial and human consequences—e.g., an attack damaging the air traffic control system might produce high costs but limited casualties—but history provides a limited basis for assessing the scale of initial damages from such an attack or the likely speed of recovery (and therefore the likely duration of system disruption).

Threat and **vulnerability** are much more problematic to assess using retrospective analysis. Though what terrorists have done in the past is useful in attempting to predict their future behavior, their ability to vary their attacks and identify new vulnerabilities means it will be an imperfect predictor. The vulnerability of the target and the consequences of attacks on it have changed significantly over the time period of the historical data, reducing confidence that future behavior will track with historical trends.[13]

However, the changes that have occurred in both terrorist tactics and security strategies with respect to aviation targets make simple extrapolation questionable. This could suggest focusing analysis on more recent attacks, though doing so requires basing analysis and conclusions on fewer and fewer data points, which could skew analysis. To demonstrate this point, we examined a subset of aviation attacks in the RAND dataset for the years 2000–2008, which includes 113 incidents worldwide. The majority of those incidents are attacks on *airports* from the outside, in striking contradiction to the reality that the vast majority of al-Qa'ida's recent attempted domestic attacks (the aviation threat that has received the greatest attention since 9/11) have been aimed at the inside of planes (an attack location that makes up a much greater fraction of the entire historical dataset). This demonstrates that a type of attack that has not been a major focus of domestic aviation security efforts is being carried out in many other places, but it also demonstrates the need for caution when drawing conclusions about threat in particular countries based on subsets of global terrorism databases. The smaller the sample size, the greater the chance that risk analysis will be skewed either by random variations in attack data or—potentially more worrisome—by purposeful adversary actions meant to shift our attention or create false assumptions about future attacks.

---

[13] In contrast, in an analysis of rail security (Wilson et al., 2007), we used historical attack data over a long time period as the basis for a qualitative risk analysis. In the case of rail systems, most targets were at the time (and still are) relatively lightly defended and had been over the entire historical period.

As a result of these concerns, simple extrapolation of risk based on historical data incident data to characterized current and future risk is not viable. However, such data clearly must inform such an assessment—terrorist organizations draw on their past experiences and existing capabilities as they plan their future operations—but reasonable approaches are needed to mine the data without analytical results being skewed by what the data cannot do.

Thinking About the Future: How Can We Reasonably Break Away from Designing Security for Past Terrorist Threats?

Because of the problems in projecting future terrorism based on past terrorist behavior, risk assessment efforts draw on a number of approaches to estimate threat, vulnerability, and consequences. Such efforts have utilized elicitation of judgments from a variety of types of experts, simulations combining insights into the functioning of current security measures against different threat types, and so on. These processes are vulnerable to the biases and assumptions inherent in any process relying mainly on human judgments, are costly to perform, and often incorporate significant amounts of sensitive data, which require protection that limits their broad dissemination and application.

To provide a fuller picture of risk, we wanted an approach to characterize future aviation terrorism threats that would address the problems associated with purely retrospective methods but would also limit the vulnerability of risk judgments to either present-day bias or intentional adversary manipulation. The two parts of that process involved (1) developing reasonable future threat scenarios and (2) applying a qualitative process for comparing and informing prioritization of scenarios that captures available risk insights and produces a result that is useful for security assessment and planning.

In past RAND efforts to assess terrorist threats to specific targets, we developed a general protocol to guide both assessment of the present and structured brainstorming about future threats. Though current threats are insufficient for characterizing prospective risk, they are the fundamental basis of that risk—representing both the targets of interest to and proven capabilities possessed by current terrorist actors. Considering future threats, the challenge is what we call "responsible use of imagination" starting from the baseline of today's threat: brainstorming to explore attack scenarios of concern but having systematic ways to flag or even eliminate those so convoluted or complex that they would be unlikely to ever be successfully implemented by any realistic adversary (Jackson and Frelinger, 2009).

To structure exploration of future threats, our protocol includes four core questions to be answered, adapted here for the aviation system:

1.   Starting from historical incidents, how have adversaries attacked aviation targets, and what might incremental improvements on or deviations from those tactics look like?
2.   What key problems have attackers encountered in attacking aviation targets in the past, and what changes could help them solve those problems?
3.   What have relevant adversaries said they want to do in the future—if such information is available?
4.   How might new technologies or weapons affect the options that adversaries have for attacking the aviation system?

This general approach is anchored in understanding how organizations innovate, a process that combines incremental change from the status quo, more radical alterations in technology or process, and opportunistic exploitation of new tools that become available (Jackson et al., 2005a, 2005b). Organizational innovation is driven by both changes external to the group and idiosyncratic internal preferences and desires, so both types of drivers are reflected in the approach. The following sections explore scenarios suggested by each of the four questions.

Innovations Based on Historical Attacks

Looking at the historical attack data, we can draw several qualitative generalizations:

1. *Though the hijacking of airliners to gain control of planes has dropped significantly over the years, it remains part of groups' tactical repertoires and a potential starting point for innovation.* The 9/11 attacks were a significant—though apparently isolated—example of innovation based on this proven attack strategy, combining suicide vehicle attacks with airliner hijacking. It is often asserted that the changes made since 9/11 have made the takeover of passenger airliners much less likely (e.g., Mueller and Stewart, 2008). Gaining control of an airliner today would require a more complex operation (e.g., breaking through fortified cockpit doors and dealing with potentially armed pilots) and the need to deal with a likely hostile passenger population (e.g., Freitas, 2012). Though the 9/11 attacks targeted dense human and symbolic targets, planes could be used against other targets (e.g., critical infrastructures) to produce larger-scale attacks.[14]

    Though seizure of a large aircraft has been made more difficult, use of a general aviation aircraft as a weapon is a potential alternative strategy. A recent DHS IG report characterized the risk from general aviation as modest for attacks on ground targets, since the payload that could be carried by such aircraft is less than established terrorist weapons, such as truck bombs (DHS IG, 2009).[15] However, such a plane could be used in an attack on a larger passenger airplane by collision or nearby detonation. Terrorists could also use general aviation aircraft for the "aerial bombing" (i.e., dropping explosives from planes). Though such operations have challenges that make success far from assured, groups have attempted such attacks in the past.[16]

---

[14] For example, concerns about aircraft impacts on nuclear power facilities (discussed in Holt and Andrews, 2009).

[15] Demonstrating that terrorists may still consider attacks with smaller aircraft even when seemingly more attractive alternatives are available, a plot involving just such an attack (on the U.S. Consulate in Karachi, Pakistan) was reportedly disrupted in 2003 (Eggen, 2003). Even reasonable and correct judgment that an attack type presents low overall risk does not mean that it will never happen.

[16] See discussion of an abortive attempt at this tactic by the Provisional Irish Republican Army in Jackson et al., 2005b, p. 135; see also the discussion of the LTTE's aerial bombing attempts earlier in this chapter.

2. *Attackers are using a variety of tactics to target airports.* Recent data show an upsurge in attacks on airports, even while domestic concern has focused on al-Qa'ida's multiple attempts to stage attacks inside planes. Because many ground-focused attacks are simpler and less logistically demanding than attacks on airplanes, groups with limited capabilities might find them relatively attractive in comparison (Jackson and Frelinger, 2009). Recent attacks have included timed bombings (e.g., the November 2008 attempted bombing of the Jolo airport in the Philippines by the Abu Sayyaf Group), armed attacks, vehicle bombs outside airports (e.g., a Taliban attack on Kandahar airport using a suicide vehicle bomb in July 2009), and rocket or mortar attacks from a distance (examples include attacks in both Africa and Afghanistan in recent years).[17]

Though airport attacks have a higher probability than other operations of producing at least modest casualties, reasonable incremental innovations based on current activities could include greater use of vehicle bombs in more direct attacks in an effort to produce higher casualties and broader use of suicide operatives to improve targeting. Other tactics that groups have used at other targets (e.g., multistage operations where evacuation from a structure is used to move people into range of another attack) could also be applied to airports in an effort to increase casualties.[18]

3. *There is potential for innovation regarding attacks inside aircraft.* Attacks on aircraft themselves remain attractive to terrorists for the same reasons they have always been—the potential for dramatic incidents that result in significant consequences. Though much of the focus has been on bombs smuggled through passenger security using different strategies of concealment, cargo bombs have remained a consistent—if episodic—part of the

---

[17] All attack examples are drawn from the RAND Database of Worldwide Terrorism Incidents.

[18] See, for example, cases of secondary explosive device use described in Jackson et al., 2007, by groups in both the UK and Israel.

threat picture. The 2010 plot by al-Qa'ida in the Arabian Peninsula to stage such an operation in a parallel way in an effort to produce a large-scale incident shows that the threat from this type of attack persists (see Loidolt, 2011, for a description). Though attackers have focused much of their innovation effort on how to beat existing security with established weapons (i.e., explosives), reasonable adaptation paths could include use of alternative methods to damage airframes in flight (e.g., incendiaries) or to injure the passengers or crew contained within (National Academies, 2006).

4. *Terrorists may engage in other types of operations that have not or have only rarely been used against aviation targets.* Though much of the focus of air security is on hijacking and bombing, there are a variety of other tactics that could be (or occasionally are) used in aviation system attacks. For example, armed assaults on airports are only a small slice of the aggregate threat picture shown in Figure 2.3. However, the recent increase in attacks in airports might be coupled with the high-profile success of some armed assault operations (e.g., Mumbai in 2008, some attacks in Iraq and Afghanistan).[19] Even a handful of such attacks would represent a significant spike for a threat that would currently be assessed as low-probability.

The conflicts in Iraq and Afghanistan have also produced tactics that could be employed in commercial aviation attacks, including the use of batteries of weapons, such as rockets and mortars, that could be used to attack aircraft on takeoff or landing approach or simpler explosive devices intended to create airborne shrapnel to target aircraft in similar circumstances.[20] Though elements of the aviation system infrastructure that have not been attacked in the past could be targets for groups sat-

---

[19] For a detailed description of the Mumbai assault, see Rabasa et al., 2009.

[20] An example of such a tactic was the attack on the Rashid Hotel in Iraq in 2003, when Deputy Secretary of Defense Paul Wolfowitz was there. The barrage of eight to ten rockets resulted in one person killed and 16 injured (Bonner and Shanker, 2003).

isfied with largely financial consequences from attacks,[21] such operations would be less dramatic than most of the aviation attacks that have been attempted in the past.

Examining existing ways groups have attacked aviation targets, we have found a number of potential incremental changes that could affect terrorist risk via several of the attack vectors shown in Figure 2.1. Alternative approaches to standoff attack could provide new ways to attack planes on or near the ground that do not rely on high-technology systems, such as MANPADs.

Solutions to Key Problems

In examining past terrorist operations against the aviation system, we identify two main classes of problems encountered by attackers. The first is posed by the existing, largely detection-based security measures intended to keep explosives and other weapons off aircraft. The template for future adaptation in this area can be seen in historical data. Historically, much of the attackers' focus has been on concealment, but other means could include acquisition of novel explosive materials, use of other modes of attack (e.g., incendiaries), or use of witting our unwitting individuals to bring weapons through less-secured entries into the aviation system.

The other obvious problem that attackers have encountered in past attacks has been the low probability that standoff attacks (e.g., rockets and mortars) will actually hit their intended target. Given the low observed hit rate for these attacks, transfer of tactics such as the use of batteries of devices discussed above (where multiple simultaneous shots compensate for low accuracy) would be a foreseeable path. Other options that would address this problem include the use of precision mortars—a relatively novel technology that is becoming more broadly deployed by state military forces—that include guidance capabilities (Bonomo et al., 2007). There are also a number of lower-technology strategies that groups might use to address their accuracy problems,

---

[21] For example, concerns regarding disruption of the air traffic control system would generally fall into this class of attack.

such as penetrating attacks through airport perimeters (like the LTTE suicide operation discussed previously) and the placement of weapons onto runways to strike at planes as they pass during takeoff and landing.

Expressed Desires of Attackers

Though direct information on attacks being considered by terrorist adversaries is usually restricted to intelligence channels and data obtained from closed sources, the nature of contemporary threats and groups' use of the Internet means that more such data are in the open and available for examination. Given the prominence of al-Qa'ida in the global terrorist threat, significant effort has been devoted to monitoring and reporting on the content of discussions that occur on Internet forums associated with that movement. On those websites, threats to air transportation are made and range from standard operations that mirror historical incidents to much more innovative—and even fantastical—attack scenarios.[22]

There is a strain of discussion on such posting boards that is focused on current security measures and their capabilities—i.e., what materials security measures are good or bad at detecting, ways weapons might be concealed, and so on. A discussion thread in October 2010 focused on ways of repeating 9/11-type attacks, which included aviation-focused scenarios (e.g., "martial arts like karate, kung fu, taekwondo and others, so as to overpower the plane's security and take over the plane and execute the operation") as well as possible alternative targets that could produce similar outcomes. Other discussions have focused on purely historical threats, such as luggage bombs in plane cargo. A more fantastical example was the suggestion made in November 2010 that al-Qa'ida train birds for use in attacks against a variety of targets, including planes.

---

[22] Selected translations of material posted on jihadist forums and posting boards are provided commercially by firms such as the SITE Intelligence Group.

New Technologies and New Opportunities

Terrorist organizations have proven adept at identifying opportunities that changes in technology can create. This has included both taking advantage of changes in the technological content of society (e.g., terrorist use of the Internet) and using new destructive technologies in terrorist operations. A look through the terrorism literature and public discussion of potential threats to aviation can identify a variety of speculation about the ways that technologies might be used against aviation targets. This has included concerns about cyber threats (e.g., whether jet onboard computer systems might be hacked or air traffic control systems taken over and false information injected) and even whether the food served on airplanes might be a vector for harming passengers.[23] Other new technologies that have received broader attention include the potential for laser illumination to injure or distract flight crews enough to cause accidents (U.S. House of Representatives, Committee on Transportation and Infrastructure, Subcommittee on Aviation, 2005). Since perimeters protecting planes and infrastructures are a key (and obvious) element of existing security measures, new technologies that provide other ways for attackers to bring weapons to these targets could enable other attack options. Examples of such technologies include unmanned air or ground systems that could operate either with guidance or autonomously in or above otherwise protected areas.

Conclusions

A balanced picture of the future risk of terrorism on aviation targets requires combining what we know of attackers' historical behavior with reasonable consideration of how the future may differ from the past. The order-of-magnitude differences that exist in consequences of attacks—with operations that could allow control of an airframe in the top tier, those which might cause potential loss of a fully loaded airframe in the second, and all others in the third—defined using historical data are unlikely to change much for future threats, though

---

[23]   See discussion in Jones, 2009; Forrest, 2008.

broader deployment of very high-capacity aircraft could push attacks with potential consequences in the second tier closer to the first. The variation of consequences across such a wide range will therefore have a strong influence on relative risk, and therefore concern, of attack scenarios. In spite of the increase in frequency of attacks on airports in recent years, they will remain less worrisome than airframe-based attacks because of their more modest consequences.

Changes in technology and attacker behavior could make future threats diverge from historical patterns. Any forecasting effort must be done cautiously, acknowledging its limitations. That said, a structured process that captures different drivers that could cause groups to change their behavior makes it possible to explore the future threat landscape in a commonsensical way that goes beyond simply unstructured brainstorming about what terrorists might do under different circumstances.

However, while any scenario developed in such an approach might be *possible*, not all possible ways that adversaries might attack aviation targets are equally *plausible*. To inform security planning—and given the irreducible uncertainties that exist about terrorist intent and capability—we need ways to compare potentially very different scenarios and think through which of them might be more worrisome than others. In past work, we have used an approach that uses the characteristics of scenarios to identify those that might be more or less of a concern (Jackson and Frelinger, 2009). Using this lens, we see that simple operations that have fewer "moving parts" (e.g., operations that only require a single attack team versus those that require multiple teams perform separate but coordinated actions simultaneously), fewer variables that affect success that are outside attackers' control, fewer technological uncertainties, and so on are of greater concern and should be a more prominent driver of security planning. Using such an approach to winnow possible futures, we find that the more fanciful scenarios can be discarded and attention focused on the subset that are more likely to succeed if attempted.

However, even if we were armed with an unrealistically complete intelligence picture about how known terrorist groups were planning to attack aviation, there would still be irreducible uncertainty about the future threat. As a result, though it is certainly possible to compare scenarios and identify those that involve more risk than others, we will never be able to accurately know the relative probabilities of different scenarios. Such future threat scenarios are therefore not a good basis for quantitative risk analysis, and challenge the successful integration of past and future threat information in cost-benefit and cost-effectiveness analysis.

That said, future threat scenarios can contribute to security planning and assessment in more qualitative ways. Such scenarios can be a tool for testing how security strategies that have been put into place iteratively in response to evolving historical threats are either well or poorly matched to address the range of futures. To the extent that hypothetical future attacks are initiated from the same points or have similar character to current threats (e.g., armed attacks inside airports)—or as changes are made in security strategies over time that can be shaped to address less certain threats as well—the risk associated with those attacks is hedged. But, if future threats are substantially different (e.g., the potential for advanced mortars to allow effective attacks on loaded planes on the ground or at takeoff from the outside), then they represent more substantial shifts in the risk environment, and changes in strategies to hedge against them would need to be considered.

CHAPTER THREE

The Costs of Security Can Depend on What Is Being Protected—and Security Can Affect Its Value

Brian A. Jackson

In considering a security measure's value, the starting point for analysis must be what that security measure costs. Without a handle on the amount of money spent, any measure of benefit will be a number in isolation: The same risk reduction might seem like a poor investment if it had a high associated cost, but a good investment if its costs were lower.

It is more complicated than it might seem to put a price tag on a security measure—or on a set of measures, such as those that make up the aviation security system overall. These costs, which are both direct and indirect and tangible and intangible, are paid by different entities and manifest over different timescales. Some costs are paid "up front" (e.g., money to purchase a new security technology), others are paid by each traveler as they travel (e.g., the time spent undergoing security screening), and still others diffuse through the economy to be paid (potentially in the near-invisible form of reduced profits) by industries and others whose activities and livelihoods are linked to the functioning of the aviation system. The *total* cost of security is made up of all these types of costs and more, making it very difficult to quantify. The reality that different parts of the costs are paid by different parties also means that the apparent cost of a security measure may be shaped by the perceptions and assumptions of the entity making the estimate. However, viewed from the most inclusive national perspective, all the costs of security—those paid by taxpayers (via government programs), by businesses, and by individuals as they travel—must be weighed against the benefits the security measure is expected to produce.

Most prominent and easy to measure among the costs are those paid by the government, which are available annually in aggregate for federal efforts overall and in policy documents for some individual measures. The TSA budget has climbed above $7 billion in recent years (DHS, n.d.), and estimates for individual technologies or projects (e.g., GAO, 2007b) can be found in the policy literature. In addition to costs at the federal level, airports and airlines pay costs associated with security measures (e.g., associated with complying with security regulations), some or all of which may be passed on to users of the aviation system (see Oster and Strong, 2008, or Seidenstat, 2004, for a review). A 2002 estimate by the International Air Transport Association put costs to airlines in the billions of dollars (IATA, 2002). Costs paid by local airport authorities vary, and systematic data are difficult to obtain. Based on searches of publicly released information, a 2009–2010 value for the Los Angeles World Airports police department was approximately $100 million and an older (2005–2006) estimate for the much larger Port Authority of New York and New Jersey exceeded $450 million.[1]

But beyond the costs with a budget line or a purchase order connected to them, there are other costs of security—ones whose effect can potentially be greater than the tangible costs of the systems or staff needed to implement them. Costs to passengers go beyond money collected through security fees or the increase in ticket prices caused by security mandates on airlines or airports. Viewing the effects of aviation security holistically, we see that the cost in the time that passengers must spend arriving at the airport early due to unpredictability in how long it will take to undergo security screening has a cost as well. Because of the number of travelers that use the system in a given year, estimates combining even modest wait times with reasonable values for business and leisure travelers' time can produce values in the billions of dollars for that less tangible cost alone.

---

[1] Weikel, 2010; The Port Authority of New York and New Jersey, 2005.

Though such estimates provide a way to estimate less tangible security costs, they do not capture *all* those costs. For example, various researchers have documented changes in passengers' preferences and behaviors regarding use of the air transportation system, at least in part due to the increased "hassle factor" associated with new security measures. Surveys at various points in the past decade have asked about reductions in individuals' travel behaviors (and future travel intentions), various researchers have examined both drops in demand for air transportation and whether diversion from aviation to other modes of transportation occurred during the period,[2] and industry organizations have argued that security-related diversion of passengers from aviation has produced substantial costs (e.g., Poole, Jr., and Passantino, 2003, and references therein; Consensus Research Group, Inc., 2010; Jones, 2010; Ito and Lee, 2005; Gkritza, Niemeier, and Mannering, 2006; Srinivasan, Bhat, and Holguin-Veras, 2006; IATA, 2002; Rossiter and Dresner, 2004; Gigerenzer, 2006; Su et al., 2009; Blakock, Kadiyali, and Simon, 2009). Some of these effects in principle come from effects of security that are more difficult to estimate than the time cost of waiting in line, such as concerns raised about the invasiveness of various search and personal scanning methods.

Note that not all security measures affect system functionality—at least not for all users or customers. For example, most checked baggage matching and screening practices (versus carry-on and passenger screening methods) would presumably have little or no effect on the perceived utility of the system from the perspective of an airline passenger. The presence of armed air marshals on flights (discussed in Chapter Five of this document) is a significant cost to the government and to airlines (since they occupy a seat that could otherwise be sold), but it does not affect passenger experience in a significant way.

Another challenge of quantifying costs that manifest at the passenger level—potentially producing changes in travel behavior—is that they differ from person to person, and therefore their average across the

---

[2] Some reports indicated larger effects on short-haul air travel routes and airports with larger portions of such flights, presumably because the net hassle-to-travel value ratio was higher (Maxon, 2011; Clark, 2009).

population could differ considerably from any single individual's value. While one person might be significantly offended or inconvenienced by a particular type of search, that same search might not bother another person at all. How the effects of multiple security measures "add up" is also potentially complex. While a single measure might not be viewed as creating undue hassle or costs, adding additional layers or increasing security intensity could increase perceived hassle nonlinearly, i.e., the perceived inconvenience caused by the two together could be greater than the sum of each of them when implemented separately. For example, passengers might have viewed walking through a magnetometer as having essentially no associated costs and a bag search producing a modest level of hassle—but when used together the perceived cost is greater than the bag search alone. Such effects could be caused for tangible reasons—e.g., the combined system creates longer delays than the bag search alone—or for intangible ones (e.g., a greater perceived intrusiveness of the two together).

Though previous efforts at security analysis have sought to capture some of these passenger-level costs and some of their effects, they have generally not done so fully. When they have, as reviewed above, the results of such measurements are difficult to link with traditional cost-benefit approaches, and it is clear that they do not always capture the totality of security measures' effects on passengers and on the societal value of the system they are intended to protect. Their results have also not always been in agreement, with some polls showing broad support for security measures that others suggest are reducing passengers' willingness to travel. Capturing these—potentially contradictory— effects would presumably be particularly important for transportation systems (including, but not limited to, aviation), where the "openness" and usability of the system by individual members of the public is a central driver of the system's societal value.

Adapting Techniques for Addressing Benefit Uncertainty in Security Analysis

The problem of uncertainty regarding the full costs of security measures in many ways mirrors a difficulty on the "other side of the ledger" for making security decisions: uncertainty regarding the risk from terrorism complicating assessment of the benefits of new security measures. While it is well established that there is some risk of terrorism that security measures seek to address, the magnitude of that risk—whether the expected annual losses from attacks are (at least in monetary terms) in the millions, billions, or even approaching trillions of dollars—is uncertain. If the true risk is low, then the potential benefits of improved security will be low—since they would be reducing a comparatively smaller risk. If the true risk is high, then even small percentage reductions in risk could amount to very substantial benefits.

To address this uncertainty, rather than seeking to calculate a single benefit value and assess new security measures against it, analysts have instead used ranges of terrorism risk values (Willis and LaTourrette, 2008; Jackson, 2009a; Stewart and Mueller, 2011). In such an approach, the costs of a security measures are compared with risk levels over a range, and at each point in the range, expressing the result in terms of "how good the measure would have to be at reducing risk" to be cost-effective. That effectiveness value determines where the measure would break even; i.e., it would reduce enough risk that its cost would be worth paying.[3] For a measure costing $1 million per year, the bar to break even would be much higher at a terrorism risk level of $10 million expected losses per year (it would have to reduce risk by 10 percent) than it would be if expected losses were $1 billion per year (a 0.1 percent reduction in risk would justify its cost).[4]

---

[3]   Doing that assessment against an annualized risk estimate—i.e., expected losses per year—also provides a way to smooth "lumpiness" in terrorist risk, since long time periods can elapse between significant attempts to stage attacks.

[4]   As discussed in Chapter One, though a security measure that breaks even by $1 might be feasible on paper, for a variety of reasons the goal would be to design security measures whose risk-reduction benefits *exceed* their costs, meaning they break even "and then some." Beyond the commonsensical goal of achieving the most results for the money, pursuing better than

Though such analyses do not provide single answers regarding the cost-benefit balance of specific security measures, they can be useful for framing choices, limiting decision spaces that must be considered, and potentially guiding actual security choices in some circumstances. Describing the use of these techniques with respect to nuclear detection capabilities and technologies, Micah Lowenthal of the National Academies framed their utility succinctly: "In cases where break-even analysis identifies meaningful bounds on decisions, that is, cases where the threshold conditions can easily be judged to exist, this approach can simplify decision making" (2010, p. 9). However, he went on to point out that it is not always possible to identify conditions for which security decisions essentially reduce down to clear arguments about the presence or absence of specific effectiveness thresholds.

This type of approach could be applied to the analogous uncertainties regarding the costs of security measures. To do so, the potential intangible and other costs associated with the reduction in the utility of the protected target from security measures would be examined over a reasonable range, with the goal of identifying where those costs could become determining drivers of whether the measures are cost-effective or not. In treating terrorism risk as an uncertain parameter to be varied, analysts use estimates of the sorts of annual losses that different types and scales of terrorism might produce (Willis and LaTourrette, 2008). To treat the less well-defined costs of security in a similar manner requires determining what ranges would be reasonable to vary them by—and ways to capture the potential escalation of those costs as security is increased.

Past efforts have examined some of these security costs using estimates for the time spent by passengers going through security. For example, if a rate of $20 per hour is used as the value of a traveler's time, then an additional wait of 10 minutes for security would have a "price" of $3.33 per traveler. If that cost was added to each of the 629 million (RITA, 2011a) trips taken in the domestic United States in 2010, that wait would account for an additional price tag of $2.1 *billion*. At a level

---

break-even performance also helps to hedge against the irreducible uncertainties in benefits and costs of security measures that are the topic of this chapter.

of an individual traveler, such a delay could be viewed as a surcharge on a ticket—and, therefore, a requirement that travelers pay a higher price for the same service. In the fourth quarter of 2010, the average price of a domestic ticket was $337 (RITA, 2011a), meaning the $3.33 time cost for our notional security measure would raise the price of a ticket by approximately 1 percent.

Economic techniques could be used to translate such price increases into predicted demand reductions. However, industry associations have occasionally published their own direct estimates of how much security measures are affecting the revenues of airlines. For example, in 2002, the International Air Transport Association estimated that lost revenue to airlines that year from the "hassle factor" associated with security was $2.5 billion (IATA, 2002). Assuming that such values are reasonable estimates, they can provide a way to think about the significance of diversion of passengers (or other customers, such as shippers) away from the aviation system as a result of security effects.

Though such estimates are a good starting point for thinking through the more intangible and implicit costs of protective measures, it is not clear that they capture the full picture. Beyond revenue from passenger fares and freight shipping fees, the commercial aviation system is responsible for substantial economic activity through the activities that passengers participate in as they are traveling and when they reach their destination. Such activities range from leisure (generally involving consumption and expenditures), use of shipped cargo (an element of many economic activities), and, for business travelers, activities involved in economic activity in other sectors.

Analysts have made estimates of the total economic value associated with the aviation system both in the United States domestically and for the world. The Federal Aviation Administration estimated that, for the 2006 calendar year, aviation "accounted for just over $1.2 trillion in economic activity, contributing 5.6 percent to the U.S. economy" (FAA, 2008, p. 2). An estimate more focused on just the aviation activities that security is likely to affect most significantly (aviation provision and use) would be $1 trillion.[5] An estimate made for the same year for the economic effect of aviation on the world economy was $3.6 trillion (Air Transport Action Group, 2008). The share for North America in that analysis was approximately $560 billion, a smaller value than the $1 trillion–$1.2 trillion estimate in the FAA analysis. The scale of the various indirect, induced, and catalytic economic effects (to adopt the terminology of the Air Transport Action Group) of aviation means that reduction in use of the system as a result of security measures will be greater than just the effects on airline or shipper revenues.

How much greater is an open question, however. Economic systems are complex—and so a drop in use of air transportation because of concerns about the hassle or invasiveness of security would not deterministically hurt all of these other economic activities. For example, if they did not fly, vacationers might stay closer to home, changing the location of their spending but not the amount. Business travelers might substitute other, potentially more efficient, ways of coordinating their activity without traveling—e.g., using online or other virtual meetings rather than gathering in person.

As a result, accepting that there will be irreducible uncertainty about how large these costs are and where they will manifest, a more approximate way of considering them would be to examine these effects more generically as resulting in small reductions in the overall utility of the aviation system. Like varying terrorism risk over a reasonable range, examining different amounts of "drag" that security measures might place on the utility of the transportation system and exploring how it could affect the cost-benefit calculus can provide helpful insights for decisionmaking.

What is the reasonable range over which to vary this potential cost? For the benefit-side assessment, different sets of assumptions about terrorist behavior and threat could be used to assist in defining reasonable end points for analysis. On the cost side, assumptions must be based on arguments about customer behavior and how great

---

[5] The $1.2 trillion estimate of total economic activity includes $190.3 billion (FAA, 2008, p. 17) associated with aircraft *manufacturing*.

an effect on the value of the aviation system different measures might produce.

For aviation, it is clear that for some transport tasks there are limited potential substitutes—e.g., the long transit times to cross oceans by ship, rather than aircraft, may exclude the former from competition for most passenger services.[6] In such circumstances, even significant direct and indirect costs from security might result only in a very small reduction in the perceived value of the commercial aviation system or, put differently, would mean that an increase in the total tangible and intangible costs of that service caused by security would be tolerated. On the other hand, there are more (and more practical) substitutes for the service provided by shorter flights, which would likely make them more sensitive to increases in security-related cost increases. As a result, treating the average effect as a relatively small across-the-board percentage reduction in the utility of the aviation system is a reasonable starting point for examining how behaviors change when that percentage is varied. This is also consistent with the numbers referenced previously.[7]

An Analytical Example Incorporating Intangible Costs Associated with Increasing Security

To make this concept more concrete, it is most straightforward to walk through an example that includes this sort of intangible costs of security in the way suggested above. Since this approximate approach seeks to capture all of the difficult-to-quantify effects of security as a single

---

[6]   There is an extensive economic literature on elasticity (the sensitivity to a change in price) of travel demand and how those elasticities vary as variables such as trip length change. Some of these analyses include (either implicitly or explicitly) time costs of travel, which are particularly relevant to the discussion here, where one driver of the effects of security on system value for passengers is the time spent waiting for and undergoing screening. For reviews of this issue illustrating both continuities and changes over time, see Jung and Fujii, 1976; Oum, Waters II, and Yong, 1992; Brons et al., 2002.

[7]   For example, the implicit 1 percent increase in the cost of a ticket from a 10-minute delay or the estimate of lost revenues by airlines of $2.5 billion (IATA, 2002), which—in a year where total revenues were $306 billion (IATA, 2009)—would correspond to a percentage reduction of approximately 0.8 percent.

"reduction in the utility of the transportation system"—which will be paid whether or not terrorists actually stage an attack—it affects cost-benefit analysis in two ways. To this point, the focus of discussion has been this reduction in utility as another type of cost of security. However, because some of the benefits of protecting a transportation system come from security's role in keeping the system up and functional after an attack, the drag that security can put on the functioning of the system also cuts into the *benefit* of protecting it in the first place. Put another way, if security makes the system less accessible and therefore *useful* compared with what it would have been in its absence, that effect reduces the future importance of protecting the system because of that reduced value.[8]

These two effects can be demonstrated using the basic equations for cost-benefit assessment for security measures. The following equation (simplified from Stewart, 2010) calculates the expected net benefit of a measure given estimates of its effect on terrorism risk and its various costs:

$$Net\ Benefit = [P_{attack} \times P_{damage} \times L] \times RR_{sec} - C_{security} + B_{nonterrorism}, \quad (1)$$

where

P_{attack} is the probability that an attack will occur in a given time period (expressed on a per-year basis to agree with annualized measures for costs and other benefits)

P_{damage} is the probability that damage will occur given that an attack has occurred

---

[8]   The idea that an intervention into a system has the potential to perturb or change the system itself is similar to the concept of the observer effect in the natural and social sciences—that the intervention to observe and measure a phenomenon itself will make a change to it. In that case, it is the act of observation that changes the behavior of either the physical or human system being studied. In this case, it is the intervention to protect the system that is the alteration. (The author gratefully acknowledges Sheldon Jacobson, who made this connection in his review of the document.)

L is the losses that will be produced (some of which will come from the attack denying use of the transportation system after it occurs)[9]

RR_{sec} is the amount the security measure reduces that risk (e.g., 10 percent or 0.1)

$C_{security}$ is the measure's annual cost

$B_{nonterrorism}$ is the value of any benefits (also on an annual basis) that security measure provides that are not related to terrorism (e.g., crime reduction at the protected airport).

Since the costs of security are expressed in dollars, everything else must be as well, acknowledging the issues associated with assigning dollar values to some attack consequences such as injury and loss of life. To be more realistic, the basic framing of this equation can be expanded to capture multiple different attack modes with different risks, different types of losses, multiple types of risk reduction by security measures, and so on. In this discussion, we will not do so, for simplicity's sake. To further simplify, subsequent discussion will also neglect $B_{nonterrorism}$.

If a security measure's reduction in the utility of the transportation system was "just another cost" of security, then it would appear as a component of the $C_{security}$ term. This would produce equation 2:

$$NB = [P_{attack} \times P_{damage} \times L] \times RR_{sec} - (C'_{security} + C_{SysFunc}), \qquad (2)$$

where the cost of security ($C_{security}$) is divided into separate terms for the component not related to the value of the system being protected ($C'_{security}$) and that related to the reduction in functionality of the system ($C_{SysFunc}$). For considering the value of a single security measure that affects a system's functionality, this only slightly more complex equation is sufficient, where the addition of $C_{SysFunc}$ ensures that this

---

[9] In the terminology of risk analysis, these are essentially the threat, vulnerability, and consequences associated with an attack on the system. Because the probability of attack is expressed on a per-year basis (and the other variables are treated statically), the product is an annualized risk/expected annual loss measure.

effect is not neglected. For simplicity's sake, we will treat the effect of a security measure on system functionality as a (small) fractional decrease in the value of the system, making it possible to substitute for the $C_{SysFunc}$ term in equation 2, producing equation 3:

$$NB^{(1)} = [P_{attack} \times P_{damage} \times L] \times RR_{sec}^{(1)} - (C'_{security} + [FR_{sec}^{(1)} \times V_{Sys}^{(0)}]), \quad (3)$$

where the superscript is added to net benefit (NB) and the RR_{sec} terms to identify that the NB calculation is for the first security measure added to the system, $FR_{sec}^{(1)}$ is the fractional functionality reduction from the single security measure (e.g., 0.01 for a measure reducing system value by 1 percent), and $V_{Sys}^{(0)}$ is the total annual unprotected value of the system expressed in dollars.

But in real-world security planning, important targets are almost never protected by only a single security measure, and policy decisions rarely start with the target having no defense whatsoever. As a result, to address more realistic circumstances, we need to capture how the situation changes for cases where we are not adding the *first* security measure but are adding *subsequent* measures—and we need ways to appropriately capture the potential for *each* of those measures to affect the value of the system being protected.

To do this, consider the simple case where we are adding a second protective measure after the first one described above. In this case, in addition to considering the functionality reduction of measure 2, we must capture the fact that measure 1—when it was added—reduced the value of the system. Since the losses from a terrorist attack are partly determined by the value of the system, the functionality reduction of the first measure reduces the value of L for the second, cutting into the value of the risk reduction from subsequent protective measures. To capture this effect, we must do for the loss term, L, what we did for the security cost term above, splitting it into two terms—one capturing losses from the direct effects of the attack and the one from the effects of the attack on the value produced by the transportation system. This produces equation 4:

$$NB^{(1)} = [P_{attack} \times P_{damage} \times (L_{attack} + L_{SysFunc}^{(0)})] \times RR_{sec}^{(1)}$$
$$- (C'_{security}^{(1)} + [FR_{sec}^{(1)} \times V_{Sys}^{(0)}]) \tag{4}$$

As we consider a second security measure, this makes it possible to capture the effects of the first on the expected benefit of the second. In cases where the first security measure reduced system functionality, it will reduce the $L_{SysFunc}$ term as the second measure is considered—since the value of the system functionality is incrementally less after the addition of security measure 1 than it was in its unprotected state. Since we are treating the effects of security measures on system functioning as small fractional reductions, we can carry through their effect on the $L_{SysFunc}$ term when assessing subsequent measures. As a result, for a two-security-measure case, the equation for the expected benefit of security measure 2, given the existing deployment of security measure 1, would be

$$NB^{(2)} = [P_{attack} \times P_{damage} \times (L_{attack} + \{L_{SysFunc}^{(0)} \times \langle 1 - FR_{sec}^{(1)} \rangle\})] \times RR_{sec}^{(2)}$$
$$- (C'_{security}^{(2)} + [FR_{sec}^{(2)} \times \{V_{sys}^{(0)} \times \langle 1 - FR_{sec}^{(1)} \rangle\}]) \tag{5}$$

where the net benefit now refers to the second measure ($NB^{(2)}$), $FR_{sec}^{(2)}$ denotes the fractional functionality reduction for the second security measure, and terms capturing the effect of the first security measure ($1 - FR_{sec}^{(1)}$) are added to both the $L_{SysFunc}$ and $C_{SysFunc}$ terms to show that the second security measure is "operating on" the system as already protected by measure 1. Equation 5 generalizes to a case for the nth security measure as follows:

$$NB^{(n)} = [P_{attack} \times P_{damage} \times (L_{attack} + \{L_{SysFunc}^{(0)} \times \prod_{i=0}^{n-1}\langle 1 - FR_{sec}^{(i)} \rangle\})] \times RR_{sec}^{(n)}$$
$$- (C'_{security}^{(n)} + [FR_{sec}^{(n)} \times \{V_{Sys}^{(0)} \times \prod_{i=0}^{n-1}\langle 1 - FR_{sec}^{(i)} \rangle\}]) \tag{6}$$

Using equation 6, we can show how changes in different parameters affect whether the net expected benefit of a security measure is likely to be positive or negative, taking into account both its effects on system functionality and the effects of security measures implemented before it. It should be noted, however, that this construction assumes independence of the two security measures—i.e., that the addition of measure 2 does not affect the functionality/value of measure 1 positively or negatively. Here we make that simplifying assumption, but in reality it will not hold—a topic discussed in Chapter Four of this document.

Effect of Security-Induced Utility Reduction When Protecting Increasingly Valuable Systems

Using equation 4, we can demonstrate the effect of security-induced reductions in the value of a system on the outcome of cost-benefit analysis for a single security measure by varying both the size of those effects and the value of the protected target. For simplicity, we hold all other parameters constant. We vary the value of the system from 1 to 100 units, where a unit could be any monetary measure (e.g., a billion dollars annually) and other effects and costs are also expressed in these relative units. We will take as our example case the following conditions:

framework would also be consistent with different users of a system having different thresholds at which the level of security changes their behavior and, as security is tightened, larger and larger fractions of the population pass their thresholds of concern.

In the simple example shown in Figure 3.2, including increasing marginal functionality costs to security to the calculation only requires adding a multiplier to FR_{sec}, where each subsequent level of security has a higher associated cost than the preceding one (in the example here, each is 1.1 times "more expensive" than the previous level). This situation, which results in nonlinearity in both the security induced cost and net benefit curve, is shown in Figure 3.3.[14]

The addition of this effect—which, while done both schematically and hypothetically here, is not unrealistic—causes the net benefits curve to bend downward as the functionality-related costs escalate. After an initial increase (when the effects of additional risk reduction still outweigh the functionality cost), the curve bends and the net benefit eventually drops below zero.

Conclusions—Consequences of Including Security-Induced Functionality Costs in Assessment

Looking at simple analyses with security-induced effects on system functionality included, can we, as Lowenthal suggested, identify "threshold conditions" that "can simplify decisionmaking"? First, based on the structure of equations 3 and 5, a security measure's effect on system functionality will generally be greatest through its contribution to $C_{security}$ versus the effect it has on the benefits of security measures—since the latter effect appears as a product with the level of

---

[14] This effect could be reinforced by the potential for *decreasing returns to additional security* measures as well—i.e., though the first "unit" of security added might reduce risk by 10 percent, the second identical unit will not produce the same marginal benefit. At the minimum, even if it is identically effective to the first, it will cut risk by 9 percent from the baseline level, since 10 percent of that risk was already addressed by the first unit. There may be other effects that create stronger diminishing returns as well. These types of behaviors are discussed in later chapters on security layering and the trusted traveler program as well.

terrorist risk to the system and the level of risk reduction of the security measure(s) being analyzed (all of which will generally be values that are less than 1). However, if terrorist risk in the absence of the security measure being analyzed is very high,[15] its other effect would become more important.

The second broad point (demonstrated in Figure 3.1) is that the more valuable the asset that is being protected, the more dominant utility reduction from security will be in the expected benefit function. In the example graphs in this discussion, one hundred units—at $1 billion each—was used as the value of the system. This is threefold below even the revenues of the aviation system, and at least tenfold below the FAA estimate of the contribution of aviation to the domestic U.S. economy. If such estimates of the total value of the aviation system and associated economic activity are used as the basis for comparison, even a small percentage reduction in system utility would represent a substantial additional cost. To calibrate, for the domestic U.S. estimates, a 0.5 percent reduction in the utility of the aviation system would correspond to either $2.5 billion or $5 billion, depending on the estimate used. These numbers are of the same order of magnitude as TSA's $5.2 billion line item for aviation security (DHS IG, 2011). Given uncertainty surrounding the magnitude of security effects on system functionality, it is not possible to provide a figure for this additional cost term—but to assume that existing passenger screening methods have reduced the value of the aviation system from what it would be in their absence by half a percentage point (or even more) seems defensible. As a result, whether explicitly recognized or not, these type of costs are almost cer-

---

[15] The structure of the equations above is based on the probabilities associated with a single attack. If there is a significant probability of multiple attack attempts in the absence of the measure(s) being examined, then reflecting that would increase the importance of the loss reduction effect. This could be done having a set of probabilities associated with different total losses (e.g., a probability of one attack resulting in a loss of L, of two attacks producing a loss of $2L$, and so on). Since the functionality reduction caused by security would affect each of those terms, the influence of that term in the cost-benefit results would multiply.

tainly a major component of the costs of some current aviation security measures.[16]

The examples presented here also help to define "threshold conditions" for where these effects are of particular importance. In the examples discussed above, relatively high rates for probabilities attack and damage given an attack (50 percent and 25 percent, respectively) and high damage values (in the billions of dollars per attack) were used. While one attack every two years has been roughly the rate of post-9/11 attacks by al-Qa'ida on the U.S. aviation system, whether the other parameters are appropriate or not depends on how a specific cost-benefit analysis was framed.

If the focus of analysis is examining the costs and benefits of a single security measure to be added to an existing baseline level of security, then the probabilities (including the risk reduction from security used in the example calculations) are likely too high.[17] Assuming that the existing set of security measures in place already substantially reduces the risk of terrorist attack on aviation, additional measures would have a much smaller RR_{sec} (since they would only be contributing to reducing the residual risk not already addressed by the existing security practices) and P_{damage} would likely be lower (since experience over the decade since 9/11 suggests that attackers' probability of success is much lower than 1 in 4). It could also be argued that the loss values used in the example calculation are artificially high, since if the annual value of aviation and its spin-off economic activity approaches a $1 trillion per year, the damage values used in our calculation would correspond to losses from an attack of $60 billion. With these values, the net benefit of additional security that reduces risk by 10 percent is positive (Figures 3.2 and 3.3, "first level" of added security), with an associated—almost minimal—assumed reduction in system utility of 0.05 percent. If that reduction in system utility increases, the high value

---

[16] As cited previously, there are many measures that—at least from the perspective of specific categories of users or customers—would not have these effects (e.g., checked baggage screening).

[17] If the intent was to examine aviation security overall, some are likely low—since without such security measures, at the minimum, the probability of attack would be much higher (as discussed in Chapter Two) and other parameters would likely increase substantially as well.

of the aviation system means that the net benefit of additional security goes negative quickly (at an effect on system utility of 0.07 percent). If any of the risk or effectiveness parameters go down significantly, the value of any additional security similarly "goes negative."

Even though this discussion was based on notional values, even such a simple calculation demonstrates the major effect that reductions in system utility—when reduced to an estimated monetary cost—can have on the cost-benefit balance of a security measure. In this chapter, no example calculation included a percentage effect on the value of the aviation system above 0.8 percent.[18] Though the amount by which any specific aviation security measures might reduce the utility of the aviation system is clearly open for debate—and different approaches could be used in an attempt to measure such an effect—the argument that measures that affect passenger or shipper experiences (or combinations of measures that do so) could have effects at the fractions of a percentage point level seems reasonable. Even at that level, the implicit cost of seemingly small percentage reductions in system functionality is substantial. Whether the value of the aviation system is set at the FAA (2008) level of $1 trillion annually, or using a smaller basis, such as total airline revenue (approximately $175 billion in 2010 [RITA, 2011a]), the resulting value can approach the billion-dollar level. Without reliable estimates of the residual terrorist risk that the measure is designed to reduce and its effectiveness in doing so, maintaining a positive net benefit in spite of such utility costs will be difficult at best.

---

[18]   After the tenth level of security was added in the calculation behind Figure 3.3, the cumulative reduction in system utility rounded to 0.8 percent.

CHAPTER FOUR

The Benefits of Security Depend on How Different Security Measures Work Together

Tom LaTourrette

A common aspect of the design of security systems is the use of multiple layers of security. The rationale for using multiple layers is that no security element provides perfect protection, and using multiple layers of different types of security elements provides protection against the inevitable shortcomings with any individual element. Shortcomings could include being bypassed through known or unforeseen gaps inherent in the design, being temporarily inoperable, or being overwhelmed or incapacitated. TSA promotes the fact that it uses a layered approach to aviation security (TSA, n.d.-b).

The rationale for security layering is similar to that for incorporating redundant elements for safety—both approaches provide backup capability in the event that one element of a system fails. As is the case with safety redundancy, security layering comes with a cost. Beyond the obvious cost of incorporating additional components (e.g., software, hardware, and staff) into a system, using multiple security layers leads to diminishing returns—continued investment is rewarded by less and less enhancement in overall system performance. This occurs because each new layer backs up an existing layer, and hence some fraction of the full benefit it would provide if it were operating by itself is supplanted by the operation of and benefit from the previously existing layer. The degree of diminishing returns depends on the extent to which security layers are redundant as opposed to complementary. Entirely redundant systems (e.g., checking a boarding pass twice) provide the least additional benefit, while more complementary systems (e.g., using x-ray and canines to screen baggage) have less overlap and hence provide more additional benefit.

Beyond the diminishing returns resulting from overlapping capabilities of multiple security layers, the benefits of layered systems may also be influenced by interactions among the layers themselves. That is, the existence of one layer could affect how another layer performs. One security element that performs in a particular way in a particular environment may perform differently when that environment is altered by the introduction of another security element. This describes a situation in which the performance of separate elements of a layered security system are not independent, but rather depend in some way on the other elements in the system. Thus, system performance in a layered system may be affected by layer interactions.

All security elements are inherently limited, and one way these limitations are dealt with is to layer multiple elements together. The value of security layering depends on the cost of each layer and the benefit each new layer adds to the overall system. The benefit, in turn, depends not only on how well the individual security elements work on their own, but also on how well they work together.

In this chapter, we first examine how different types of security elements operate and how layered security systems can be distinguished based on the types of security elements they comprise. We characterize security elements in terms of important functional attributes and discuss how different types of layers can be combined to maximize overall system performance. We next examine the question of how individual security layers interact and how these interactions could enhance or degrade the performance of individual layers and the overall system.

Dimensions of Security

A helpful starting point in understanding how to assess the effectiveness of a layered security system is to distinguish security elements according to how they complement each other and interface with each other. Different types of security efforts can be distinguished in a number of different ways:

- the types of attack pathways the security measure protects against
- the security method and its effect on an attack
- the extent to which the security effort operates passively versus requiring active participation of security staff or passengers
- the extent to which it relies on human decisionmaking versus technical automation.

Where a security element lies along each of these dimensions can influence how and how well it integrates with other security elements.

Attack Scenarios and Pathways Protected Against

Few, if any, individual security elements protect against all threats to the aviation system. While a wide range of aviation attack scenarios are possible, there are relatively few pathways by which terrorists or weapons reach their targets (see Chapter Two). Security elements can therefore be distinguished according to the attack pathway in which they operate. In the realm of aviation security, attacks can be perpetrated by using a number of different pathways, including passengers, employees, food, carry-on luggage, checked luggage, cargo, ground vehicles, standoff delivery, and control facilities.

These pathways cover most of the weapon-target pairings considered to be of greatest concern in aviation security—weapons such as bombs, guns, and standoff weapons (including rockets, mortars, and high-powered rifles), and targets such as aircraft, aircraft flown into buildings, people in airports, and airport structures. As discussed in Chapter Two, a single attack may involve more than one pathway, and some pathways can be used in multiple types of attacks (e.g., a passenger can hijack a plane to use as a weapon, carry a bomb onto a plane, or carry a bomb into a terminal). In addition, more exotic pathways, such as remotely piloted airplanes, could add to the threat in the future.

When examining a set of security measures as a layered system, what is important is how the layers that are relevant to particular attack pathways interact. Layers that cover different pathways (e.g., identification checks at an employee entrance to an airport versus the screening done of passengers before boarding) may be part of an overall security strategy, but a single attacker who has adopted a single attack pathway will only "see" one of them, and so their performance will not interact or reinforce each other in the same way that two layers on the same pathway would.

Security Method

Terrorist attacks are often thought to involve a series of planning, reconnaissance, and execution actions. This provides the opportunity to intervene at multiple stages using different types of security methods. Some security efforts attempt to deter attacks before they are carried out, while others are designed to interdict attacks in progress. We can define four general types of security methods: those that deter, detect, deny, and engage. Deterring entails causing the adversary to voluntarily withdraw from a specific attack plan. Deterrence is based on adversaries' perception of capabilities, and deterrence can be engendered through deception even when actual capabilities are quite limited. Detecting refers to observing and recognizing a potentially suspicious or dangerous person, activity, or material. Denying is administratively or physically limiting progress of a person, activity, or material (with or without retaining it) before harm has been incurred. Engaging refers to halting an attack in progress. Broader security planning also covers response and recover measures after an attack, but they are not treated here.

Security elements can be classified according to the method by which they act. The extent that a particular security measure will deny an attacker depends on the characteristics of the attacker: For example, a fence could completely stop some attackers but merely slow down others that have the capability to breach the barrier. In addition, many security elements fall into multiple categories. For example, virtually all security acts as a deterrent in addition to whatever else it may do. Nonetheless, recognizing this distinction can help better understand the mix of different methods and their effects that are included in a layered security approach.

Passive Versus Active Security

Different types of security entail differing amounts of active involvement from the people involved—passengers, security staff, or other employees. Some security elements are entirely passive, meaning that they operate without any sort of regular actions or inputs. Most measures thought of as mitigation fall into this category. Examples include structural hardening of buildings or cargo containers, bollards, and fences. Other security elements, such as pat-downs and explosives trace detection, are completely dependent on active steps taken by all participants. Still others lie somewhere in between. For example, door locks passively prohibit unauthorized entry but require security staff to lock the door. Passive systems have the advantage of being more robust—they are always operating and, because they are independent, are less vulnerable than active systems to performance degradation from administrative decisions, staffing shortages, power outages, network problems, or failure of external systems. On the other hand, the capabilities of passive systems are limited.

Human Versus Machine Decisionmaking

While a complete security system will nearly always include some degree of human decisionmaking, some individual elements may operate entirely automatically. A walk-through metal detector, for example, automatically determines whether a person is carrying a metal item that exceeds the detection threshold and, if so, sounds an alarm. While the alarm resolution typically requires human actions and decisions, the actual detection does not. Detection of suspicious behavior by a behavioral detection officer, on the other hand, depends entirely on human decisionmaking. The extent to which security relies on human or machine decisionmaking depends on the status of technology and evolves over time. For example, until relatively recently, video surveillance relied on human viewers to detect objects or events of interest. With the rapid advancement of video analytics, however, more such decisions can be made by machines. Machine decisionmaking is more robust because it is not vulnerable to staffing issues, variations in worker skill levels, or lapses in attentiveness. On the other hand, many security decisions require complex judgment and are beyond the capabilities of machines.

Combining Security Elements to Cover Dimensions

The classification of security elements according to these dimensions may provide useful insights for designing layered security systems and for characterizing their performance. An effective security system will need to cover all the pathways by which terrorists may attack. Considering how security measures span potential pathways of interest will help identify potential gaps. In addition, mixing different security methods will likely make a security system robust against variations in adversary tactics and unintended gaps or shortcomings in individual security elements. Finally, there are some important advantages of passive over actively managed security and of machine-based over human-based decisionmaking. While there are limitations to what is currently possible with passive and machine-based security, and such approaches are subject to some important vulnerabilities, incorporating these approaches in a security system provides robustness in the face of vulnerabilities posed by shortcomings in infrastructure and staff.

Performance of Layered Security Systems

The performance of a layered security system will depend not only on the inherent performance of the individual elements of the system, but also on how interactions between those elements may alter their inherent performance. Security layers can interact in a number of ways. In some cases, the performance of one element may depend on the detection outcome of another element. For example, the probability of an alarm in a layer can depend on whether or not there was an alarm in a prior layer. This situation was examined by Kobza and Jacobson (1996), who show that the effect of layer dependence on system performance depends on two key system design choices: the criterion for when a second security layer is used (always, periodically, or conditional on an alarm in a prior layer) and how a system alarm is defined (if any layer gives an alarm or if all layers give an alarm). They identify the conditions under which a system with dependent layers performs better than a system with independent layers. For example, the probabilities of false clears and false alarms are lower when the probability of a false alarm in layer 2 decreases given a false alarm in layer 1, and the probability of true alarm in layer 2 increases given a true alarm in layer 1. In other words, the system performs better when layer dependency allows the second layer to perform better than it would when layers are independent.

In general, however, simply the operation of an additional security element can influence the performance of individual elements and hence the performance of the system overall. There are a number of ways in which the presence of multiple security elements, regardless of whether or not any triggers an alarm, can affect the performance of one or more of the individual security elements. In some cases these effects stem from aspects of how the security elements themselves interact, and sometimes the interactions also involve how an adversary responds to the combination of elements.

Such interactions can work in either direction. Separate security elements may combine in such a way that the total system effectiveness is enhanced relative to the case when elements operate independently. Alternatively, security elements may interfere with each other or be susceptible to failing in related ways such that the system effectiveness is degraded relative to the elements operating independently.

In this section, we discuss several ways in which this type of interaction could occur. The interactions we examine comprise a mix different effects, including layer performance being dependent on the detection outcome of a prior layer, the existence of another layer, the susceptibility to related failures, an adversary response, and whether the interaction enhances or degrades system performance relative to the layers operating independently. Our objective is to identify the types of interaction effects one might expect to see in layered security systems, often drawing on experience from safety systems. There is little documented evidence of interaction effects in layered security systems. Thus, while in some cases we note relevant implications from quantitative modeling, our emphasis is to qualitatively describe possible interactions to focus future modeling and data collection efforts.

Interactions That Enhance System Performance
Complementary Capabilities

Multiple layers can complement each other, adding more to system performance than each layer individually. This is the case for detection technologies, such as video surveillance. By itself, detection of a potential threat does little to reduce risk beyond some level of deterrence. Only when detection is combined with an alarm resolution layer that involves denial or engagement does the combination of security elements provide substantial benefit. Similarly, while denial could, in principle, be applied randomly with some minimal effectiveness (in practice, this would of course be unacceptable), it is far more effective when informed by a detection step.

Detection layers can also complement each other by targeting different regions of a detection regime, such as mass, size, or material type. This narrows the spectrum over which each individual layer must focus, allowing layers to target particular regions. For example, walk-through metal detectors and body scanners provide complementary detection capabilities with regard to bombs. In combination with a metal detector, a body scanner can be designed to place less emphasis on identifying, for example, concealed wires, such as might be used in a detonator.

Information Transfer

Another way in which multiple security layers can reinforce each other is when information gained from one layer is used to enhance the performance of another layer. This is an example of dependencies that affect layer performance being conditional on whether an alarm is triggered in one layer. An example of this is a procedure used by some airlines in which results of interviews with passengers are used to optimize the seating of federal air marshals. If a passenger interview results in suspicions exceeding some threshold, the airline will seat a federal air marshal near that passenger to increase the probability that the marshal will be able to successfully intervene if an attack begins. The effectiveness of the air marshal in that case is greater than the effectiveness of the air marshal without the interview. If enough interviews are conducted for there to be a question or concern about a passenger for each flight with an air marshal,[1] then this increase would apply to the entire air marshal program.

Increasing Deterrence

A final way security layers might reinforce each other is if they combine to exceed an adversary's threshold for deterrence. For example, an adversary concerned about arousing suspicion because of nervousness or other anomalous behavior might feel capable of successfully transiting a passenger security screening checkpoint, but may decide that the combination of a checkpoint plus behavioral detection officers throughout the airport makes risk too great to warrant an attempt. Similarly, a terrorist carrying a weapon may feel able to pass through a single checkpoint but might not be willing to risk the combination of checkpoint followed by additional security screening in the gate area.

In such cases, combining layers does not influence the performance of the individual layers relative to the layers operating individually. But when the combined performance exceeds the adversary's deterrence threshold, the benefit of the layers transitions from one based primarily on detection and denial to one based on deterrence.

Interactions That Degrade System Performance

Lulling

Perhaps more commonly than providing an extra boost in security performance, there are a number of ways in which multiple security layers can interact to erode performance of individual layers. One way this occurs is through the lulling (also referred to as shirking) effect. Lulling refers to decreasing the level of care being exercised with a particular safety or security element when a redundant element is introduced. This is an example of dependencies that affect layer performance being conditional on the presence of other layers, regardless of the alarm status of any layer. The typical situation in which this effect occurs is the introduction of a regulatory or engineering intervention that leads to individuals being less careful than they were before the intervention

---

[1]   The fraction of flights in the U.S. that have air marshals is not public information, but is estimated to be less than 10 percent (Stewart and Mueller, 2008).

(e.g., Pitzer, 2005; Johnston, 2010). Viscusi (1984), for example, identified this effect for aspirin: When child-resistant caps were introduced, adults were less likely to replace the cap and put the bottle out of a child's reach. Although we are not aware of empirical evidence for the lulling effect in security, the combination of machine technologies with hand-searching and human perception is the type of environment in which lulling could conceivably occur. For example, the introduction of body scanners may lead transportation security officers or behavioral detection officers to be less attentive in identifying unusual behavior or as vigilant in searching.

Offsetting Behavior

A second way additional layers can erode expected system performance is through offsetting behavior (also referred to as risk compensation or risk homeostasis, Wilde, 2001). Offsetting behavior is closely related to lulling in that the addition of new safety or security interventions causes participants to exercise less care. However, offsetting behavior entails participants deliberately engaging in more risky behavior that offsets the benefit of the safety intervention. As with lulling, the best empirical evidence comes from safety. Offsetting behavior is documented in areas ranging from food safety (Nganje, Miljkovic, and Ndembe, 2010; Miljkovic, Nganje, and Onyago, 2009), automobile safety (Peltzman, 1975; Sobel and Nesbit, 2007; Jorgensen and Pedersen, 2002), and occupational safety (Bridger and Freidberg, 1999).

The case for overcompensation in security is more speculative. In security operations, for example, in addition to preventing dangerous materials and people from passing through checkpoints, operators also have incentives to minimize delays and to provide a nonintimidating, nonconfrontational experience for passengers. The introduction of body scanners could cause security screeners to feel that they do not need to be as vigilant and can therefore shift more of their attention to increasing throughput or better interactions with passengers. This could reduce their ability to detect dangerous materials.

Interference

A third way in which interactions among security layers might degrade performance relative to layers acting independently is when layers indirectly interfere with each other. This could occur if the introduction of a new security element increases the background signal level ("noise") relevant to another security element. For example, the prospect of being subjected to enhanced pat-downs may raise the anxiety or agitation level for all passengers, which would make it more difficult for behavioral detection officers to detect the anomalous behavior characteristics of potential terrorists.

Another way security elements could interfere with each other is if an element requires more resources than anticipated, for example, by generating a large number of false alarms. Resolving these alarms would create a burden on security staff that could reduce their effectiveness in operating other security elements.

Still another type of interference could be caused by active participation from an adversary. If an adversary was able to exploit some aspect of a security element, such as a detector or security officer, to cause a distraction and draw attention, this action might divert or deceive other security resources and leave alternate paths more vulnerable than they would otherwise be.

Insider Threat

A fourth way in which additional security may not raise overall system performance as much as expected is by increasing the probability of insider threats (Sagan, 2004). As security resources (e.g., the number of security guards at a nuclear power plant) increase, the probability of an undetected insider threat on the security force increases. This argument differs from the preceding points because the addition of security does not diminish the effectiveness of existing security layers. Rather, the threat in this case is that, as the number of security forces increases, the number of insiders increases to the point where insiders can defeat the overall security system. This argument could apply to any size security force. In small security operations where the baseline insider threat is convincingly zero, additions to the security force will raise the probability of an insider threat from zero to nonzero. On the other hand, if the insider threat depends on the absolute number of insiders, large operations may be particularly sensitive to hosting a critical number of insiders.

Related Failure

An important consideration in designing redundant safety and layered security systems is understanding how system elements fail. If multiple system elements can fail in related ways, then the benefit of redundancy or layering can be compromised. The safety literature identifies two types of related failures: cascading (or induced) failures and common external cause failures (Yellman, 2006).

Cascading failure is when failure of one element of a system causes the subsequent failure of another element. An example of cascading failure of redundant safety systems would be if an engine on a multi-engine airplane disintegrates and releases material that subsequently destroys another engine. Failures can also cascade more indirectly, such as if an engine becomes damaged or fails and the pilot accidentally shuts off a different engine (Yellman, 2006). Cascading failures are also common among linked elements that manage a flow or load (e.g., electrical power transmission or financial systems).

In the context of aviation security, cascading failure is probably not a major problem in most circumstances. For example, the failure of a behavioral detection officer to detect a terrorist presumably has no effect on the probability that the terrorist's weapon would be discovered at the passenger-screening checkpoint. Further, security layers are typically designed to account for failure of prior layers. For example, armed air marshals are prepared to confront armed hijackers on airplanes, who could only be present if the passenger screening checkpoint layer failed to detect a weapon. Cascading failure could occur if scanning equipment failed and all passengers and luggage had to be hand-searched. The increased burden on security staff could lead to performance degradation of hand-searching.

Common external cause failure is when a single causal factor external to the system leads to failure of multiple elements of a system. In the realm of aviation safety, common external cause failure is much more common than cascading failure. Yellman (2006) cites numerous known examples for airplane engines, including failing to load enough fuel for a flight, improper maintenance of engines or fuel systems, volcanic ash or birds getting ingested into engines, and unusual air turbulence.

For security, common external cause failure could occur if an adaptation made by an adversary in response to security resulted in the defeat of multiple security layers. This may involve an operational innovation, such as a new weapon design that eludes all current forms of detection. Or it may be a more fundamental change in approach that defies basic assumptions on which current security designs are based. This is, to some extent, what led to the success of the 9/11 attacks. At an operational level, the aviation security system performed as it was designed. The failure was that the adversary used an approach that was not accounted for in the system design. Consequently, all security layers failed to prevent it.

More general types of external causes that could affect multiple aviation security layers are failure of power or communications systems, fires or natural disasters, or conditions leading to worker fatigue or poor morale.

Implications for Assessing Benefits of Aviation Security

Our examination of how separate security elements work together in a layered system suggests some implications for assessing the benefits of aviation security. Security layers can be distinguished according to some key characteristics, and the overall performance of a layered security system can be maximized by combining security elements in ways that span these characteristics. The benefit of a security system will therefore depend on the extent to which the layers use differing security methods, address differing attack pathways, and comprise automated and passive approaches. The more different each layer is from the previous layers, the greater the probability of success in preventing threats that reach it. Such a system is more robust against a wider range of types of attacks and a wider range of possible failure modes than one that consists of largely redundant elements.

However, even in the most robust design, layering provides diminishing returns because layers are often partially redundant and additional layers protect against more and more unlikely threats. This is a fundamental argument against a stance that more is always better.

In a carefully designed system, some layering is beneficial, but the marginal benefit of additional layers eventually decreases to the point where including them is not worth the cost.

Finally, when combining security elements in a layered system, it is important to consider the ways in which separate security elements might interact with each other, either in a synergistic, security-enhancing way or in a counterproductive way in which overall security is less than expected. We have identified several ways in which security elements might interact to produce such unexpected results. Most of these interaction modes have been observed in the context of safety. While a reasonable argument can be made that they are also relevant to security, they have only been documented anecdotally in a security environment (Johnston, 2010). Consequently, it is difficult to predict the extent to which certain security elements or combinations of security elements might be particularly susceptible to certain types of interactions.

Even if we know an interaction effect can occur, it would be difficult to estimate its magnitude. In principle, effects could be so large as to cause a system to "backfire," meaning that the performance degradation resulting from combining multiple layers is great enough that adding additional layers actually decreases overall system performance relative to a nonredundant system (Sagan, 2004). While such extreme negative interactions may require extrordinary circumstances (Yellman, 2006), even much more modest interaction effects can result in significant unanticipated lapses in security performance that can result in increased costs, increased uncertainty, and increased risk.

CHAPTER FIVE

The Benefits of Security Depend on How It Shapes Adversary Choices: The Example of the Federal Air Marshal Service

Russell Lundberg and Tom LaTourrette

Introduction

To understand the full benefits of a security measure, we need to capture how it changes adversary thinking. Terrorists are adaptive adversaries, so the addition of a security measure may change what or how a terrorist attacks. The United States can meet its goal of decreasing the damage we can expect from attacks by decreasing the likelihood an attack will be undertaken, decreasing the likelihood an attack will succeed if it is undertaken, and decreasing the damage that occurs if the attack succeeds. A central effect of security is deterrence, which increases security by making terrorists less likely to attack or inducing them to switch to an attack that is less likely to succeed or that, if it does succeed, has lower consequences.

Deterrence is harder to assess than many other benefits of security measures. To think through how to do so, we will look at one security measure that is designed to have a significant effect through deterrence, the Federal Air Marshal Service, and explore how to capture deterrent effects in the analysis of the benefits of a security measure.

The Federal Air Marshal Service is one of the innermost layers of aviation security, providing the capability to interdict attacks in progress on planes. There are other layers of security at the plane level (including hardened cockpit doors and armed flight deck officers) and several before reaching the plane (including passenger screening and checkpoints). Armed and undercover federal air marshals (FAMs) present an active layer of security, available to respond to and potentially preempt attacks, including both 9/11-style cockpit assaults and some kinds of bombings. Although information on the actual number of FAMs is not publically available, it is estimated as being only a few thousand, covering only a small fraction of the total flights, perhaps 5 percent (Elias, 2009; Hudson, 2004, 2005; Meeks, 2004; Meckler and Carey, 2007).

Estimating the costs and benefits of FAMs has several challenges in common with other aviation security measures. It is only one layer of a larger security system, making it difficult to attribute security improvements to one layer or another, particularly when deterrence is involved. Additionally, the risk is due to an intelligent adversary that will seek out the weakest points of the system. As a related point, we cannot be certain of the likelihood and consequences of attacks that would occur without security measures in place, so estimating the reduction in risk is often challenging and open to debate.

There are also important ways in which FAMs differ from many other aspects of aviation security. First, FAMs operate near the final phase of an attack scenario by actively engaging terrorists during an attack. This differs from most other security, which is based on detection and denial earlier in the attack scenario. They also have the capability to be reactive to a threat rather than only presenting a static defense. Second, as compared with perimeter security measures, such as reinforced cockpit doors and passenger checkpoints, FAMs do not *directly* protect all airplanes. FAMs are only present on a small number of planes, prioritizing high-risk flights. However, they are on these planes undercover, and attackers cannot be certain which flights they are on. This provides some expectation of security as perceived by the attackers, as attackers cannot be certain whether or not a flight is protected until the attack is revealed. This expectation is likely to be strongest for those high-risk flights prioritized by FAMs, but there is at least a possibility of FAMs on any flight. This perception of security may change the attackers' choices, creating additional security for flights with no marshal present through deterrence. In this way, while the *marshals* themselves cover only a small number of flights, the *Federal*

Air Marshal Service as a whole can be seen to some extent as covering them all.

These challenges complicate efforts to estimate the benefit of FAMs in reducing risk. Yet at the same time, measures of costs and benefits are needed to help inform government investment decisions. We consider an approach that examines the benefit of FAMs in light of the uncertainties; we do not necessarily present a "best" estimate, but instead identify the range of conditions under which the benefit of FAMs would exceed the cost to see whether they are plausible.

How Effective Do FAMs Have to Be at Reducing Attacks?

Defining a Risk-Reduction Threshold

To examine the conditions under which the benefits of FAMs match their costs, we use a break-even analysis. This entails setting annual benefits equal to annual cost and then examining conditions required to maintain that equality. While FAMs may provide benefits in addition to increased security (such as maintaining public order on the aircraft or reassurance as to safety), we will limit our consideration of the benefits of FAMs to their contribution to aviation security.

If the benefit of security is the value of losses from terrorist attacks avoided because of the security, equating benefits with costs gives

$$(L_o - L_{FAM}) = C, \tag{1}$$

where L is loss, C is cost, the subscript *FAM* is for the case with FAMs, and the subscript *o* is for the case without FAMs, and losses and costs are annual amounts. Following Willis and LaTourrette (2008), we define a dimensionless risk-reduction factor, $R = (L_o - L_{FAM})/L_o$, which represents the fractional extent to which FAMs reduce risk. Substituting this into equation 1 gives

$$R = C/L_o. \tag{2}$$

Annual terrorist attack losses are the product of the annual probability of an attack, P, and the consequences, or damages, of an attack, D, giving

$$R = C / P_o D_o. \tag{3}$$

Equation 3 relates the risk reduction from FAMs to their cost and the consequences and annual probability of attacks they prevent. While expected values of risk reduction should not be the sole basis for decisionmaking, particularly with the large uncertainty of estimates that are evolving over the time periods required for risk-reducing investments to pay off, they can be useful to set up a discussion informing the debate. This equation allows us to identify a minimum risk reduction for which the benefits of FAMs equal their cost.

Data Used for Estimating Hijacking-Style Attacks and Bombings

The break-even risk reduction defined by equation 3 depends on a number of parameters. The cost of FAMs is fairly well defined. We limit ourselves to consideration of direct costs and omit externalities (such as airlines having one fewer seat available on some flights). Federal budget figures show requested budgets somewhat over $900 million per year for FAMs, and actual expenditures just under $900 million per year (OMB, 2010). We round this figure to $900 million per year for the cost of FAMs.

Attack probabilities and consequences are much more poorly defined, so our analysis explores ranges in these parameters. FAMs may be useful under two different scenarios of airline attacks. The scenario with larger consequences is a hijacking-style attack, similar to the 9/11 attacks, in which the airplane is hijacked and used as a missile against another target. Scenarios of hijackings in which the plane is landed and terms are negotiated are not considered here; not only are the physical damages and lives lost much smaller than when the airplane is used as a missile, but the frequency of negotiated hijackings declined in recent decades even before the increased security following 9/11. The second scenario is to bring down the plane in midair with a bomb smuggled into the passenger cabin. There are conceivably other ways in which terrorists could attempt to bring down a plane in midair from the passenger cabin (e.g., toxic chemicals), but it is unclear how FAMs would reduce these risks. Regardless, there are two main consequence categories for commercial aircraft—using an airplane as a weapon and destroying a plane in midair—and we can include novel but unlikely approaches in these categories.

The probability of an attack if FAMs were not present is highly uncertain. As only one hijacking-style attack has occurred, estimation of a trend is based on a single data point, one that does not reflect current security measures. So rather than use a single estimate that may or may not be correct, we consider a range of estimates. We start with a baseline likelihood of 1 attack every 10 years suggested by Stewart and Mueller (2008), but also present half (1 in 20 years) and double (1 in 5 years) that estimate for comparison.

For bombings, we also consider multiple probability estimates. There have been three known attempted bombings in the passenger cabin of airplanes in or coming to the United States, suggesting 3 in 10 years as one estimate. However, there are reasons to argue that the number of expected attacks could be higher or lower. On the one hand, none of these attempts succeeded, suggesting that the probability of *successful* attacks over ten years is lower. On the other hand, there were three attacks while FAMs were in place, and we do not know how many attacks FAMs deterred. Lacking better constraints, we consider probabilities for bombings for 0, 3, and 6 attacks in 10 years.

The expected consequence of an attack is composed of loss of life, property damage, and indirect consequences, such as short- and long-term business losses. We present the expected consequences measured in dollars, so they are directly comparable to the expected costs of FAMs. Estimating the number of lives lost results in some uncertainty. We have only the events of 9/11 to estimate the number of lives lost in a hijacking-style attack. There are reasons to believe that the 9/11 attacks may represent a worst-case scenario, and the difference between a first attack and an additional attack may be significant (Mueller, 2002; Seitz, 2004). Still, this is our one observation from which we can extrapolate. Approximately 1,000 people were killed, on average, for each plane that reached its target. The consequences of another successful hijacking-style attack might range between hundreds and thousands killed. The typical number that would be killed in a bombing is less uncertain and largely reflects the number of people on the plane, which can range up to a few hundred on the larger airliners.

To make these deaths comparable to the costs, they need to be valued in terms of dollars. While the value of a statistical life can be debated, it is typically valued between $1 million and $10 million. We use an estimate from Robinson et al. (2010) identifying $6.5 million as an appropriate measure for the value of a statistical life with regard to homeland security deaths.

Lives are not the only source of loss in a terrorist attack. In addition to the direct physical damages of the attacks, we may also consider business disruption, lost productivity and spending, and loss of confidence in the financial markets. Researchers have estimated the costs of the events of 9/11 in many ways, leading to a range of estimates. Modeling approaches and studies of financial markets (representing a perfectly adaptive market economy, where damage in one area is balanced out by investment in another area) suggest no economic damage (Stewart and Mueller, 2008), while considerations that include expenditures of additional security and international wars in addition to physical damage and business interruption lead experts to estimate damages in the trillions of dollars (Mueller and Stewart, 2011). Typical estimates focus on the physical damages and business disruption due to the 9/11 attacks, with costs ranging from tens of billions to 100 billion dollars (Gordon et al., 2007; Thompson, 2002).

The economic damages of a bombing are estimated to be much lower; we use an estimate of $1 billion per fully loaded airplane lost to explosion (Chow et al., 2005; see also discussion in Chapter Two). The uncertainty in the estimated damage of an airline bombing is similar but proportionally smaller than in the case of a hijacking-style attack.

Results Find a High Bar for FAMs to Break Even

Using equation 3 and the ranges of values presented above, we can identify the break-even threshold for the benefit of FAMs to exceed their costs under scenarios for hijacking-style and bombing attacks.

CHAPTER SIX

The Benefits of Security Depend on Tradeoffs Between Intended and Unintended Consequences: The Example of a Trusted Traveler Program

Edward W. Chan, Brian A. Jackson, and Tom LaTourrette

Over the years, more and more measures have been put in place in an effort to increase aviation security. One of the most visible aspects of aviation security is the physical screening of passengers at the airport. Attempted attacks, and the uncovering of other threats, have resulted in an ever-increasing amount of resources devoted to screening passengers, along with an increase in the burden on passengers in terms of time, convenience, and invasiveness of screening. Whether these security measures are effective and an efficient use of resources is often debated.

A criticism that is often leveled is that such security measures are applied evenly across all passengers, without regard to an assessment of the risk profile associated with the passenger. A targeted approach, so the argument goes, would improve security and/or reduce costs by focusing screening resources on those passengers judged to be higher risk, while relieving the burden on those judged to be lower risk. This would require a system that can identify the risk posed by each passenger.

Trusted traveler programs represent one approach to segmenting the passenger population by risk level. Unlike negative profiling approaches,[1] which seek to identify passengers deemed to be high-risk, a trusted traveler program is "positive profiling"—identifying passengers who are deemed to be low-risk. Passengers who choose to apply for trusted traveler status would volunteer to undergo a background check. Those who pass the check, and are therefore deemed to be trustworthy, would be allowed to undergo less screening at airport security checkpoints, thus relieving these low-risk passengers of some of the screening burden by offering faster and less invasive screening, and potentially shorter security lines.

While proponents of a trusted traveler program often focus on the convenience benefits to the passengers holding such status, trusted traveler programs also present the potential for security benefits. The screening resources that would be freed from screening trusted travelers could instead be applied toward screening the general passenger population. For example, more time might be spent scrutinizing x-ray images or searching bags in public screening lines. More screening staff or equipment might be devoted to running detection tests for explosives. Overall security for all passengers would thus be increased, without requiring an increase in the total amount of resources devoted to screening.[2]

Whether such security benefits can be realized, however, would depend on terrorist abilities to exploit or defeat the trusted traveler program. It would surely be tempting for attackers to attempt to gain access to the trusted traveler lines, where passengers undergo less screening at checkpoints. A terrorist group could recruit a confederate with a clean background to apply for trusted traveler status, deciding that any risk of discovery in the background check process was outweighed by the prospect of infiltrating the trusted traveler population and thus having an easier time smuggling weapons through the security checkpoint.

---

[1] For example, Reddick, 2011; Cavusoglu, Koh, and Raghunathan, 2010; McLay, Lee, and Jacobson, 2010; Press, 2010; McLay, Jacobson, and Kobza, 2008; Persico and Todd, 2005; Caulkins, 2004; Yetman, 2004 (and references therein).

[2] Background checks for clearing applicants to trusted traveler status do represent an increased cost, but such costs could potentially be borne by the trusted travelers themselves through a program participation fee.

It is this concern that has led authorities to be reticent about offering trusted traveler programs that involve significant screening reductions. When programs have been considered, they have generally not involved substantial reductions in screening for trusted travelers.[3] A security measure whose benefits vary depending on the actions of the attacker—particularly given uncertainties about attacker behavior—may at first glance appear to not be a useful program. However, with analysis, it is possible to weigh the risks and benefits of a trusted traveler program. In this chapter, we demonstrate a simplified approach to assess the potential security benefits of a trusted traveler program. We then show how attacker attempts at compromising the program affect those security benefits.

Potential Benefits of a Trusted Traveler Program, Assuming No Compromise by Attackers

To analyze trusted traveler programs, we used a simple model of the structure of a generic program. In our model, the traveling population is composed of two types of people: some small percent of the people are terrorists, while the rest of the population (the vast majority) we will simply call the general public. The trusted traveler program is voluntary, so some fraction of the public will apply, and some fraction of terrorists may choose to apply as well.

Applicants go through a background check.[4] Ideally, a background check would accept all members of the (nonterrorist) public

---

[3]   See the testimony and discussion in U.S. House of Representatives, Committee on Homeland Security, Subcommittee on Economic Security, Infrastructure Protection, and Cyber Security, 2005. CLEAR, a trusted traveler program administered by the private sector, did not involve different screening processes for its members. During the period in which this analysis was performed, the TSA began pilot-testing a trusted traveler program called PreCheck that provided somewhat reduced screening (or, put more accurately, the probability of somewhat reduced screening).

[4]   The way we have structured this model is somewhat different from TSA's PreCheck program. In that program, there is not a separate application and background check component. Rather, individuals who have been deemed trustworthy for other criteria (e.g., an existing background check through the Customs and Border Protection Global Entry program) can

who apply and grant them trusted traveler status, while rejecting all terrorists. In practice, however, some fraction of the (nonterrorist) public applicants will be incorrectly rejected. Likewise, some fraction of the terrorists will be incorrectly accepted into the program. For simplicity, we assume that terrorists who are rejected from the program are not jailed (since the nature of most practical background check processes for such a program would not result in the certainty required to act against an individual), but instead return to the general population and travel with other members of the public who either have been rejected from the trusted traveler program or have chosen not to apply.

At the airport, passengers will go through security lines, where they will receive some amount of security screening. Under the scenario where a trusted traveler program exists, those with trusted traveler status are granted access to special trusted traveler security lines,[5] where they will go through a reduced amount of security screening relative to the amount that is currently performed. The rest of the travelers go through the public security lines.

We assume that the reduction in screening for trusted travelers allows some amount of security resources to be freed. In our analysis, these resources are all redeployed to the general public lines. Consequently, travelers going through the public security lines will receive an increased amount of screening relative to the amount that is currently performed. Figure 6.1 shows the schematic of the application of members of the traveling population to become trusted travelers.

We model this shift in screening resources as being cost-neutral. (For simplicity, we will not count background check or other program costs; some or all of these costs may be borne by applicants to the trusted traveler program. Here we are focusing on screening resources.) The easiest way to think of these resources is as time spent on screening passengers. Minutes of staff time reduced in screening trusted travelers

---

participate, but members of the general public do not have the option of separate application to the trusted traveler program itself. See TSA, n.d.-a.

[5]   Trusted travelers would be issued credentials to access a separate screening area. Such credentials would likely include biometric identification to make it difficult for one person to exploit another's trusted traveler status.

Together, these factors determine the number of terrorists who will be in the trusted traveler screening line, and subject to the reduced chance of being caught, compared with the terrorists who are in the general public screening line.

With these factors in mind, it is possible to analyze the increases or decreases of security that would result from implementing a trusted traveler program. The results will depend on the values of these factors and how they interact with one another. We can compute, for various combinations of factors, the number of terrorists who successfully pass through passenger screening with a weapon, and thus determine how much a trusted traveler program will help or hurt security under different sets of conditions. The process for doing so is easiest to demonstrate with a numerical example.

In recent years, the number of "traveler trips" in the United States has averaged approximately 625 million trips per year.[8] Suppose that the number of trips in which terrorists attempt to breach security with a weapon is 125 trips per year. (For this example, we selected an intentionally high number, since it reduces the need to talk about "fractional terrorists," as we did in the example above in which we used only 10 attackers.)

As a baseline, let us assume that the trusted traveler program is not in place and that current screening performance is 60 percent effective. Under this scenario, security screening will catch 60 percent of the terrorist attempts to board with a weapon. Thus, 50 terrorists per year would succeed in breaching screening.

If a trusted traveler program is then implemented, we can use our model to determine how it will affect this number of "terrorists through security" under different conditions. To keep this discussion simple, we will set as constant the performance of the background check for being accepted as a trusted traveler and assume, due to cost concerns, a moderately effective check that (correctly) rejects 70 percent of terrorists who apply, thus (incorrectly) accepting 30 percent

---

[8]   Since a traveler passes through security each time he or she takes a single trip in one direction, we use "traveler trips" per year in the analysis, not individual travelers. If one person takes 10 trips in the year, that person would account for 10 traveler trips.

of terrorist applicants. We will also assume that this same check will (correctly) accept 80 percent of nonterrorist applications while (incorrectly) rejecting 20 percent of nonterrorists who apply. Some fraction of the public chooses to apply for trusted traveler status. The number of trusted travelers will, along with the amount of reduction in screening applied to each trusted traveler,[9] affect the amount of screening resources that will be shifted from trusted travelers to general public screening, increasing security. In addition, some fraction of terrorists will also apply for trusted traveler status, which will decrease security.

Figure 6.4 shows how the performance of a trusted traveler program varies as a function of the fraction of the traveling public that chooses to apply for the program[10] and the fraction of terrorists that attempt to infiltrate. The green shaded area shows the region in which the combination of public participation and terrorist attempts to infiltrate trusted traveler results in a reduction of terrorists who succeed in penetrating screening. The top of the green shaded area in each graph shows the best possible performance (i.e., the amount of screening is reduced to the perfect amount within our modeled range to achieve

---

[9] Determining the amount of screening reduction for trusted travelers requires its own analysis of tradeoffs. A larger reduction in screening for trusted travelers results in more resources that can be freed up for screening the general public. This increases the chances of catching terrorists in the general public traveler line, but at the cost of decreasing the chances of catching terrorists within the trusted traveler line. The optimal split in screening will depend on the expected fraction of trusted travelers who are terrorists versus the fraction of general public travelers who are terrorists. In practice, these numbers will not be known and, moreover, will vary as the fraction of public participating in trusted travelers varies. However, for purposes of analyzing the performance of a trusted traveler program, we have assumed that these figures are known and that the optimal screening reduction is selected, thus giving the trusted traveler program the benefit of the doubt. Readers interested in more details of this analysis should be referred to Jackson, Chan, and LaTourrette, 2012.

[10] In our analysis, since the focus is on actions at the security checkpoint, the value of most interest is the fraction of the traveler trips (defined above) by applicants to the trusted traveler program. As a result, one individual (if he or she is a frequent traveler) could account for a larger percentage of the traveler trips than the percentage he or she represents of the "people who traveled" in a given year. Jackson, Chan, and LaTourrette, 2012, discuss this issue at length.

Conclusion

Trusted traveler programs have the potential to improve security. Unlike some other security measures, the amount of security improvement depends on decisions by the travelers: the decision by the general public to apply for trusted traveler status and the decision by terrorists to (hopefully not) apply. Because such decisions are out of the control of the security agencies, and yet have the potential to affect the success of the security measure, security agencies have thus far been reticent to offer such programs.

However, it is possible to quantitatively analyze the costs and benefits of programs even in the face of such uncertainties. By varying the values of the unknown parameters, we can identify conditions under which a trusted traveler program will be attractive (such as high public participation) and those under which it will be unattractive (such as high terrorist infiltration). The knowledge that a 50 percent public participation rate could improve security regardless of terrorist infiltration can give program designers confidence in the usefulness of a trusted traveler program, as well as impetus to encourage high public participation. Conversely, the knowledge that at a rate of 25 percent public participation the program will be successful only if few terrorists apply can encourage the design of disincentives (for example, the potential for a terrorist applicant and his or her confederates to receive more focused law enforcement attention or even be arrested if they fail the background check, rather than simply returned to the general traveling population pool).

The analysis in this chapter demonstrates two important points. First, decisions that are made by others can have an impact on the effectiveness of a security option. This includes not only decisions made by potential attackers in attempting to infiltrate a trusted traveler program, but also decisions by members of the general traveling public to apply as well. Second, even when the benefits of a security option depend on actions taken by others, it is still possible to analyze the security consequences. Too often, the uncertainties will cause policymakers to throw up their hands and simply opt for the most risk-averse strategy (such as allowing for no reduction in screening even for trusted travelers). While this may be prudent in some situations, the chapter shows that even with uncertainty, an analysis that considers a wide range of parameters can show the limits of the worst-case scenario, as well as point to strategies that can be used to shape adversary as well as general public behavior that push the cost-benefit balance back in the security planner's favor.

Epilogue: Considering the TSA's PreCheck Program

During the same period that this analysis was performed, the TSA developed and pilot-tested a new program called PreCheck, providing the potential for some screening reduction for some portions of the traveling public. That program differs in some respects from the way our model is framed here; in the interests of applying our results to the current program, briefly considering those differences and their implications is worthwhile.

First, unlike our model, PreCheck—at least at the time of this writing—does not have its own background check process that any member of the public can apply for. Instead, populations who have already received some types of background checks (e.g., through Customs and Border Protection's Global Entry program) are eligible for trusted status, as are some very frequent flyers identified by individual participating airlines (TSA, n.d.-a). As a result, rather than there being a single background check of specified quality as we have modeled, acceptance into the program is determined by a set of separate "background checks" with differing characteristics and, therefore, differing false positive and negative rates, which would complicate the simplified depiction shown in Figure 6.1. The lack of a route for public applications for trusted status reduces the fraction of the traveling public that could participate in the program, but at the same time *may* reduce the opportunity for attackers to attempt to gain trusted status.

Second, the reductions in screening for individuals granted trusted status also have been modest to date. The changes have included keeping more clothing on and removing less from carry-on luggage before x-ray screening, but still undergoing some technological screening

(TSA, n.d.-a). Though converting those procedural changes to a percentage reduction as we modeled here is not straightforward, it is difficult to argue that it is anywhere near the 50 percent reduction we have used in our example here. TSA also has included in its procedures that even members of the trusted traveler program are not guaranteed expedited screening, i.e., they can be randomly sent through the general public lines, further reducing the potential for resource reallocation from the trusted to nontrusted populations as we have modeled the process.

Whether changes will be made in the future that broaden the ability of members of the public who are not already participants in an existing program to participate is unknown. If it did so, then PreCheck would become more similar to the model we have described here. To the extent that existing programs like Global Entry remain the path for members of the public who are not frequent flyers to participate, then the characteristics of that background check—and the possibility for terrorists who are threats to aviation security to pass that check—will become the parameters of interest for this type of modeling. In any case, as the implementation of PreCheck continues and experience with its outcomes can make it possible to better understand not just background check performance but how much resource reallocation it enables and its effects on security for screening members of the general public, this type of modeling could contribute to adjusting and improving the program over time.

CHAPTER SEVEN

Can the Benefits of Security Be Estimated Validly?

Andrew Morral[1]

Previous chapters in this book highlight how aviation security analysis should conceptualize risk, using information about threats, vulnerabilities, consequences, and the costs and benefits attributable to security systems. These discussions raise a question that has challenged DHS since its inception: How do we estimate these components of risk given the profound uncertainties inherent in each? Congress, the Office of Management and Budget, GAO, and legislation require DHS to produce risk and risk-reduction estimates, but they also criticize DHS methods for generating risk estimates that fail to account for known or suspected complexities in terrorism risk (e.g., Masse, O'Neil, and Rollins, 2007; GAO, 2009a).

Thus, a trend at DHS has been to develop increasingly complex models of terrorism risk, like the Risk Analysis and Management for Critical Asset Protection, Risk Analysis Process for Informed Decision Making, Biological Threat Risk Assessment, Maritime Security Risk Analysis Model, and many others (Masse, O'Neil and Rollins, 2007; National Research Council, Committee on Methodological Improvements to the Department of Homeland Security's Biological Agent Risk Analysis, 2008b; National Research Council, 2010). Some of these tools attempt to estimate terrorism risk from first principles, modeling the effects of adversary preferences, decisionmaking, and capabilities

---

[1]   Portions of this chapter also appear in *Modeling Terrorism Risk to the Air Transportation System: An Independent Assessment of TSA's Risk Management Assessment Tool and Associated Methods* (Morral et al., forthcoming), which was developed in conjunction with this chapter.

on attack behavior, in addition to comparably detailed modeling of the likely performance of security systems, the likely direct effects of successful and partially successful attacks, and the cascading economic, political, and psychological effects of attacks.

The complexity of these risk models makes them less transparent than earlier, simpler models that worked from rough aggregate estimates of threats, vulnerabilities, and consequences. With the loss of transparency, important questions have been raised about the validity of current terrorism risk models and what role they can be entrusted with in homeland security planning. For instance, in its 2010 study of risk modeling at DHS, a National Research Council panel reported that "with the exception of risk analysis for natural disaster preparedness, the committee did not find any DHS risk analysis capabilities and methods that are yet adequate for supporting DHS decision making, because their validity and reliability are untested" (National Research Council, 2010, p. 2). The panel went on to recommend that "DHS should strengthen its scientific practices, such as documentation, validation, and peer review by technical experts external to DHS. This strengthening of its practices will also contribute greatly to the transparency of DHS's risk modeling and analysis" (p. 3).

In this chapter, I argue that complex, "high-resolution" models of terrorism risk play a vital role in

- developing our understanding of terrorism risk, including its characteristics and uncertainties
- helping to focus our intelligence efforts on information that will be useful for improving understanding terrorism risk
- specifying the characteristics of low-resolution models that are appropriate for supporting policy decisions.

High-resolution models can be useful for these purposes without being valid for predicting terrorism risk or for estimating the risk reductions that security measures are likely to offer. Instead, high-resolution models need to be sufficiently credible and useful to promote insight, experimentation, and exploration that supports simpler, low-resolution analyses that can aid DHS leadership to understand how their policy and resource allocation decisions are sensitive to factors that are not yet well understood, and to defend these decisions when they are scrutinized by Congress, the Office of Management and Budget, the public, or other oversight authorities.

Risk Model Validity Depends on the Intended Uses of the Model

Validation of complex models has been a key concern of the military simulation community for over three decades. Since 1991, the Military Operations Research Society, MORS, has organized a series of "SIMVAL" (simulation validation) workshops on this topic, and other researchers, vendors, and organizations too have tried to clarify what it means for complex simulations to be valid, and under what circumstances they can be found to be so (e.g., Davis, 1992; Ritchie, 1992; Hodges and Dewar, 1992; Dewar et al., 1996; Hartley, 1997; Bigelow and Davis, 2003; Pace, 2004; Chaturvedi et al., 2008; Hodges, 1991; Sargent, 2005). Much of this work has been done by RAND, and so I draw heavily on our own work for this discussion.

Department of Defense Instruction 5000.61 defines model validation as "the process of determining the degree to which a model and its associated data are an accurate representation of the real world from the perspective of the intended use of the model." In other words, a model may be valid for one set of uses but invalid for another. In addition, validity requires not just a model capable of accurately describing the world; input data required by the model must also be accurate. We know how to accurately model an arrow's flight, for instance, but without input data on its speed and direction, our analysis will be invalid for predicting where it lands. If the model or the data it uses are not accurate, its results may be completely wrong, so the uses for which the model can credibly or validly applied are narrow.

There are distinct validity criteria for different classes of uses (Dewar et al., 1996). At a high level of abstraction, we distinguish between three classes of uses for simulation models, each requiring different validity criteria. Strongly predictive models, the first class of use, are those designed to mirror reality with known precision. When models or analyses are used to predict the future on high-stakes questions like "Will the astronauts be safe?" or "Will the multimillion-dollar security program reduce risk?" this represent a class of uses with the most demanding validity requirements (Dewar et al., 1996). Predictive validity requires that both the model and its data accurately describe reality.

As in the case of complex meteorological models, strongly predictive models need not be consistently accurate, but validation requires understanding the distribution of prediction errors expected for the model (Dewar et al., 1996). Therefore validation requires a strong basis in settled theory and a sufficiently large empirical basis for judging the model's reliability. This is a standard that terrorism risk models cannot hope to achieve.

For some phenomena, such as the weather, there are enough data to compare results from different models to hundreds of historical events with roughly comparable input conditions. The same is not true for terrorism, which has as many critically important input factors to consider but a comparative poverty of historical evidence. Even for air transportation terrorism, which has a reasonably large number of historical events (see Chapter Two), changes in security environments, terrorist groups, their objectives, and their tactics result in very few events that share enough similarity to provide a set of test cases for any particular set of model inputs.

A second class of model uses involves understanding phenomena, refining theories and analysis strategies, supporting exploratory modeling (discussed more later), generating new insights, and recording, preserving, and conveying knowledge. When the conceptual models underlying these simulations are good, they can be predictive if accurate input data are available. When conceptual foundations are less well developed, these models can support theory development for complex phenomena by promoting rigorous and detailed analysis of what is and is not known about the modeled phenomena.

For instance, consider a model designed to account for how risks might shift to less well-defended targets after introduction of a security countermeasure. The process of designing such a model can trigger important conceptual developments concerning how adversary resources and capabilities affect such shifts, about adversaries' utility functions (What are the range of objectives they might have? Do they pursue optimizing or satisficing outcomes?), about how imperfect information or predispositional biases might affect target choice, etc. Working through such considerations can result in new, possibly testable theories of adversary behavior.

A third class of uses involves informing policy decisions. These models are specifically designed to address the major factors affecting decisions under consideration, and they are designed to help decisionmakers understand how important sources of uncertainty affect the likely outcomes of their decisions. That is, these models are designed to support exploratory analysis (Davis, 2002). For instance, by exploring modeled outcomes across the range of possible values on uncertain input variables, it might be possible to establish the conditions under which a new security technology appears to be effective and those under which it does not. In contrast to strongly predictive uses, for which the most likely outcome is calculated, exploratory analysis can be used to understand the range of possible outcomes given sources of deep uncertainty in either the input data or the conceptual model. Such analyses are particularly valuable for decisionmakers who recognize that they cannot predict future conditions with accuracy and therefore wish to select policies that are robust across the range of plausible futures.

Validation of analytic methods for exploratory uses does not necessarily require demonstrating predictive validity. Nevertheless, trusting a model to correctly reveal how key uncertainties could affect outcomes requires a strong, credible conceptual model for which any uncertainties in, for instance, causal relationships can be thoroughly explored, and for which data used as inputs (as opposed to those that are treated as sources of uncertainty) are accurate.

As such, establishing the utility and credibility of analyses used for exploratory analysis requires assessing the credibility of the conceptual models and input data used to support them, and carefully documenting the assumptions, uncertainties, and conjectures on which any predictions rest. Tools using rigorous data and conceptual models can be said to be valid for exploratory analyses. As the credibility of the conceptual models or the data decline, the utility of the model for exploratory analysis suffers.

Models that are clearly unsuited to exploratory analysis (too many variables, too many uncertainties) often serve other critical functions. High-resolution models can drive development of improved conceptualization of complex phenomena for analysts and leadership, by promoting rigorous and detailed analysis of what is and is not known about the modeled phenomena. By identifying important factors that may not have been previously considered, such model development can help to inform analysts, decisionmakers, and the low-resolution models that can be used to rigorously evaluate policy options. Insights from these models can also help identify data requirements that can be used to focus intelligence collection or research efforts.

Using this classification of intended uses for terrorism risk models at DHS, we suggest that DHS and TSA should work with their high-resolution models to develop low-resolution models useful for exploratory analysis, theory development, and the generation of new insights on risk management.

Terrorism Modeling Requirements for TSA and DHS Decision Support

Major acquisitions, strategic planning, and most resource allocation problems require decisionmakers to anticipate possible future conditions and how candidate policies or investments might perform under those conditions. If predicting the future were easy, or just a matter of plugging the right starting values into a well-constructed model, planning would be easy. But even when current information is very good, such as the data we have on financial markets, our success in predicting the future is poor, and models attempting to forecast the future are often subject to profound and structural sources of uncertainty that can bias predictions in unanticipated ways. This may be especially true when models are designed to predict the behavior of small groups of terrorists, some of whom we know little or nothing about today, whose motivations, intentions, capabilities, and organizations are evolving and who are studying our defenses to design attacks to circumvent our security using carefully planned surprises and innovations.

Deep uncertainties about future terrorism, like uncertainties about future stock market conditions, favor decisions that offer robust performance across diverse possible futures, rather than selecting investments that optimize performance but only for a particular future. In the language of decision theory, policymakers seek strategies that are flexible, adaptive, and robust (FAR strategies; Davis, Shaver, and Beck, 2008) to hedge against major uncertainties. Flexible strategies are those that can simultaneously address multiple requirements or objectives, including some that were not anticipated; adaptive strategies that can anticipate and build in approaches for modifying or changing their approach in response to new information or conditions; and robust strategies that can perform well or resiliently after adverse shocks.[2]

Modern decision-support tools aid decisionmakers in understanding how their options are likely to perform across a range or spanning set of scenarios selected to highlight how deep uncertainties in our current understanding of the future could affect which decisions are best. Deep uncertainties differ importantly from statistical uncertainties, which can often be estimated when well-understood phenomena are subject to uncertainties with probability distributions known through repeated observations. Deep uncertainties, in contrast, exist where we lack vital information about the phenomena under investigation, the mechanisms that produce them, how parameters interact with each other, and the true values or distributions of those parameters (Davis, Kulick, and Egner, 2005).

Examples of decision-support methods designed to address the effects of deep uncertainty on investments, policy, or strategy include Scenario Planning (Schwartz, 1996), Alternative Futures Analysis (Slaughter, 2005), Capabilities-Based Planning (Davis, 2002), Portfolio Analysis (Davis, Shaver, and Beck, 2008), Assumptions-Based Planning (Dewar et al., 1993), and Robust Adaptive Planning and Robust Decisionmaking (Lempert, Popper, and Bankes, 2003). Each

---

2   In some contexts, a "robust" strategy is considered one that includes all of these features. The word "robust" has different meanings in English.

of these methods seeks in different ways to understand the range of possible futures, how they relate to multiple objectives, and the policies or investments that offer the most robust benefits across objectives and divergent futures.

When models are subject to deep uncertainties about the mechanisms producing modeled outcomes, or the input conditions affected by those mechanisms, exploratory analysis can be used to systematically look across as many combinations of parameter values as necessary to understand not an average expected outcome, but rather the input conditions under which the model produces qualitatively different outcomes.

As noted earlier, the trend across DHS has been to develop high-resolution models, many of which depend on speculative theories of adversary behavior and intentions and the judgments of intelligence analysts and subject-matter experts to supply parameter estimates for which there are no credible sources of information (National Research Council, Committee on Methodological Improvements to the Department of Homeland Security's Biological Agent Risk Analysis, 2008b), and which often involve dozens, hundreds, or thousands of input data values, many or most of which are estimated imprecisely.

These conditions, paired with the unavailability of empirical data against which to compare model predictions, often make these models poor tools for exploratory analysis and inadequate for advising policymakers, who need to reason about issues and can do so only with a modest number of variables (e.g., 3–12, not hundreds). Even where computers could efficiently explore a larger parameter space, the complexity of results exceeds what a decisionmaker can understand and explain effectively. Because these tools must support high-stakes decisions that are subject to intense public and oversight scrutiny, it is essential that they be transparent and easily explained (Bigelow and Davis, 2003; National Research Council, Committee on Methodological Improvements to the Department of Homeland Security's Biological Agent Risk Analysis, 2008b; National Research Council, 2010). It will not suffice for the policymaker, or those he or she reports to, to justify decisions with an unvalidated model that is a black box, or even with a validated model but unvalidated and unvalidatable input data, even if it is clear that the box was created by talented analysts.

In summary, therefore, to provide credible support to decision-makers, policy models must highlight how sources of deep uncertainty might affect outcomes and decisions, they must be transparent, and they must be explainable (Bigelow and Davis, 2003). These requirements all argue for "low-resolution" models: models that do not attempt to resolve the phenomena into fine distinctions but instead consider broader, more general factors that plausibly represent the principal factors affecting the policy or decisions.

Such low-resolution policy models typically extract no more than 10 or 12 parameters that can be easily explained, understood, and used to highlight basic tradeoffs as they occur across a spanning set of possible future scenarios (Bigelow and Davis, 2003). For instance, whereas the details of how the United States might structure its military forces and systems to provide the nation with the ability to rapidly strike any target around the world (that is, a global strike capability) might entail thousands of assumptions, caveats, parameters, and contingencies, at a high level, the major tradeoffs between alternative force structures can be characterized simply, and usefully, for major investment decisions (Davis, Shaver, and Beck, 2008).

In the next section, we offer an illustrative example of how deep uncertainties might be explored in a low-resolution model of aviation security risks.

An Illustrative Low-Resolution Model of Aviation Security

At the more detailed, high-resolution level, there are hundreds or thousands of sources of deep uncertainty:

- How do different terrorist groups value production of death, economic losses, media attention, political influence, or psychological effects, and what determines these preferences?
- What resources and capabilities will future terrorist groups enjoy, and what factors determine whether they can acquire them?

- How much can these groups learn about our defensive systems and capabilities, and how do they collect this information?
- Under what conditions do our systems perform well and poorly?
- How will terrorists innovate to circumvent our systems, and how quickly?
- How will our systems evolve in response to future threats, and how will that evolution affect the usefulness of security programs currently under consideration?
- How should we estimate the cascading economic consequences of successful attacks, let alone the psychological and political ones?
- Will future attacks trigger policy responses, such as aviation system shutdowns or wars, that must be predicted to understand the risk and risk reduction?

These and many other questions for high-resolution models quickly overwhelm our ability to develop easily understood, transparent models useful for exploratory analysis, much less models that can stand up to rigorous validation. At a much lower level of resolution, however, useful generalizations of the deep uncertainties can be developed that are fairly comprehensive but more manageable for understanding and communicating tradeoffs.

To illustrate, suppose our objective is to provide decisionmakers with useful information for deciding whether to invest in a new security program that could reduce the likelihood of one type of attack, called Attack C. To achieve this objective, our analysis needs to provide a credible conceptualization of the decision problem that is transparent, easily explained, and highlights how major sources of uncertainty affect the decisionmakers' choice about the new security system. Suppose, too, that we are reasonably confident about the direct costs, in lives and damage, that each of five attacks might produce (Table 7.1), but judge that important high-level sources of uncertainty remain for the following:

- *Indirect economic effects of terrorist attacks.* Whereas models exist for the effects of security and attacks on the aviation industry (Peterson et al., 2007), a broader view of the economy is likely to see compensatory growth in other parts of the economy when air travel declines, and the cascading economic effects of such large shifts in economic activity like this represent a notoriously complex problem (Enders, 2007). Moreover, since choice of attacks depends on the adversary's perception of and preference for indirect effects, even the best available economic models of indirect costs may be poor proxies for attacker judgments of these effects. Therefore, in our illustrative example, we explore the effects of deep uncertainties in indirect economic effects by considering a range of such costs that span more than an order of magnitude (Table 7.1).

- *Attacker capabilities.* Although we have good intelligence on the aspirations and capabilities of some threatening groups, we have little information on the capabilities they may have over the lifecycle of candidate security measures. Moreover, there may be other groups or individuals with capabilities we are not yet aware of. For these reasons, attacker capabilities represent another key source of uncertainty that we represent in our model as probabilities of success, ranging from incompetence (almost no chance of success) to highly competent attackers (Table 7.1).

- *Deterrence.* Homeland security executives know little about the deterrence effects of security systems, other than that deter-

Table 7.1
Illustrative Data for Low-Resolution Model of Air Transportation Security

Attack	Deaths	Direct Costs ($ millions)	Indirect Costs ($ millions)		Terrorist Capabilities (probablity of success)		
			Low	**High**	**Low**	**Medium**	**High**
A	1,000	100.00	500	10,000	0.01	0.20	0.50
B	500	30.00	100	9,000	0.05	0.40	0.75
C	500	3.16	20	7,000	0.20	0.50	0.80
D	100	3.00	50	8,000	0.25	0.60	0.85
E	75	2.00	50	1,000	0.30	0.70	0.90

Expected Consequences of Succesful Attack

rence effects are vitally important (Morral and Jackson, 2009). Because so little is known, DHS models often ignore the possibility that attacks will be deterred. In such models, attacks might proceed even if the probability of success is small. In contrast, Enders and Sandler (2006) provide evidence that terrorists may require as much as a 75 percent chance of success in order to proceed with a difficult attack, such as one involving hostage-taking. Clearly, therefore, deterrence effects represent a key uncertainty for understanding the effects of any new countermeasure. For our illustrative analysis, we consider three levels of deterrence effects: no deterrence effects, medium deterrence effects (attackers are deterred from any attack with 25 percent or lower chance of success), and high (attackers are deterred from any attack with 50 percent or lower chance of success).

Additionally, we assume that the attacker values each death at $7 million and seeks to maximize expected losses, which can be expressed as the sum of losses from deaths, direct costs, and indirect costs multiplied by the probability of success. Both of these assumptions, and others too, could also be treated as sources of deep uncertainty, but to simplify this example we treat them as known. Similarly, we make the simplifying assumption that all costs and benefits can be monetized. In fact, some of the "value" produced by different attacks may not be easily or correctly monetized. However, low-resolution models can be extended to describe multiple objectives, rather than the unidimensional one we use here for illustration.

Using the data and assumptions described above, Panel 1 of Table 7.2 shows how the three major sources of uncertainty affect what we believe attackers currently view as the most attractive attacks in the absence of the new technology, meaning the attacks that produce the greatest expected losses. Across the parameter space defined by our uncertainty variables, our low-resolution model shows that there are conditions under which all five candidate attacks might be preferred by some attacker, with the lowest-capability attacker preferring the less consequential and easier Attacks C, D, and E, although if low-capability attackers are subject to high deterrence effects, they would select none of the five attack options. The medium-capability attackers

onto alternative attacks in response to the new security program, and (3) does so with fairly modest and transparent speculation on how attackers might go about making such decisions. Specifically, Panel 3 of Table 7.2 shows the reduced losses associated with the change in attack preferences from before (Panel 1) to after the introduction of the new security measure (Panel 2). As expected, there are many conditions in our uncertainty parameter space under which the new program offers no benefits (red cells in Panel 3).

In addition to offering a simple and transparent method for explaining how risk reduction is likely to accrue from the introduction of a new security system, the low-resolution model offers decisionmakers a candid assessment of how deep uncertainties affect the decision at hand. For instance, Panel 3 of Table 7.2 highlights that the new technology makes unequivocal sense only if we are designing it for terrorists with mid-range capabilities who are not easily deterred by the risk of failure (green cells in Panel 3). However, if we think terrorists view indirect economic effects as quite low (or, equivalently, that they value these effects less than deaths and direct economic effects), then the program could also make sense for undeterrable low-capability attackers or easily deterred high-capability attackers as well (yellow cells in Panel 3).

Which of these conditions represent true current and future threats cannot be determined by the analyst with current data and information, so the model should not be presented to decisionmakers as the single best judgment from bad data. Instead, the decisionmaker needs to understand what we know well, what we know poorly, and how the decision could be affected by uncertainty in the latter. The low-resolution model described here offers a means for communicating this information in a credible and candid way. Finally, a key feature of this type of low-resolution model is that it can be easily implemented in a spreadsheet, allowing analysts to evaluate multiple security options quickly.

The Role of Higher-Resolution Models in a Multiresolution Modeling Program

Whereas the transparency and face validity of low-resolution models make them good for supporting policy decisions and for communications with external stakeholders, this does not mean that the kinds of high-resolution models developed across DHS have no value for decisionmaking.

As Bigelow and Davis (2003) suggest, decision support often benefits from multiresolution analysis capabilities. Whereas low-resolution models are often useful for communicating the effects of uncertainty and high-level tradeoffs affecting a decision, high-resolution models can be useful for calibrating the low-resolution models and for ensuring that a low-resolution model adequately captures important features of reality. When a decisionmaker or oversight authority asks why the adversary's probabilities of success used in the low-resolution are bounded as they are, for instance, results from the high-resolution model might be among the data referenced to explain that decision. Similarly, where the high-resolution model produces results that are inconsistent with those expected by the low-resolution model, this divergence can sometimes be useful for identifying errors in the assumptions or structure of one or both models.

High-resolution models can provide insights into the multiple ways that important outcomes that are summarized in low-resolution models might occur. For instance, in our example low-resolution model, the estimated effect of the new security measure was that it halved all probabilities of success. This judgment may reflect an aggregation of many diverse instances of risk reduction that a high-resolution model could help to enumerate and explore.

Finally, high-resolution models can often suggest key sources of uncertainty that might not otherwise be considered important for the low-resolution model. For instance, Bigelow and Davis (2003) provide an example in which detailed study of the results of a high-resolution military simulation revealed the importance of an unexpected set of variables, which, once identified, could be usefully and credibly incorporated into a low-resolution model.

Summary

High-resolution models of the type widely developed at DHS can provide value in understanding terrorism risks, but they cannot be validated for predicting future risks or the benefits attributable to new security systems. Because terrorism is evolving and there are few instances with which to compare the models' predictions, they will never meet scientific standards of predictive validity. As such, if they continue to be used to justify or explain DHS decisionmaking, it is likely they will continue to be found unacceptable by oversight organizations and scientific review groups. Worse, they might contribute to unwise or inefficient security policies.

At the same time, high-resolution models are quite useful for developing analysts' and decisionmakers' understanding of risk, for supporting and developing low-resolution models that can support decisionmaking, and for generating new insights about the nature of risk or the information that DHS should be trying to collect to better understand risk.

In many ways, therefore, I am suggesting an idea similar to one Francis Kapper offered to the Department of Defense on how it should use combat simulations three decades ago:

> The most appropriate and valid objectives for using war games and simulations within the DoD [Department of Defense] context are to: better understand complex phenomena, identify problems, evaluate alternatives, gain new insights, and broaden one's perspectives. The least valid or appropriate objectives for using war games and simulations are to predict combat/crisis outcomes or control broad and highly complex programs. (Quoted in Hartley, 1997, p. 929)

This is a view that has broad support in the community of researchers involved in military simulations, yet these uses are sufficiently valid and beneficial that high-resolution military simulation continues to be used extensively by the Department of Defense.

Similarly, we believe the high-resolution models developed at DHS could well provide useful information and insights but should not be used as decision-support tools. Instead, analysts should use high-resolution models to develop transparent low-resolution models that can be used to communicate risk and the effects of deep uncertainties about risk to decisionmakers and oversight authorities.

CHAPTER EIGHT

Conclusion: Efficient Security in a Time of Fiscal Pressure

Brian A. Jackson and Tom LaTourrette

The aviation system has been a target of terrorist attention and attack from the beginning of the era of modern terrorism. In the 1960s and 1970s, attacks on aircraft put terrorism on the international policy agenda and were central in attempts by small violent groups to gain leverage over individual governments or the international system more generally. The September 11, 2001, terrorist attacks redefined the threat of terrorism for many individuals and catalyzed rapid and sharp changes in aviation security policies across the world. Threats to the aviation system have continued in the decade since, with Richard Reid's attempted "shoe bombing" in December 2001, the 2009 Christmas Day bombing plot, al-Qa'ida in the Arabian Peninsula's failed cargo bombing operation in October 2010, and the group's subsequent bombing operation that was disrupted in May 2012.

The threats of the 1960s and 1970s laid the foundation for the aviation security system that we have today, with hijackers who could successfully commandeer an aircraft with guns or grenades resulting in passenger screening that seeks to keep weapons off aircraft. Later, explosives attacks, such as the destruction of Pan Am Flight 103 over Lockerbie, Scotland, resulted in explosives screening and other baggage-focused security measures. Though it has often been said that the 9/11 attacks changed the whole landscape of terrorism and counterterrorism, the approaches taken to aviation security in the years since have had much in common with those taken before them—with a focus on new screening technologies to defeat ever-morphing threats. Though

substantial organizational changes have been made, such as the forma-
tion of DHS and the federalization of functions that once were performed by others, the general strategy of aviation security since 9/11 is
more similar to than different from what came before.

One important difference, however, is that the cost of aviation
security has significantly increased. Before the 2001 attacks, the central federal actor in aviation security was the FAA (Krause, 2003), and
federal budgets for aviation security (and transportation security more
generally) fell in the comparatively modest range of the low hundreds of
millions of dollars (Johnstone, 2006), in contrast to the billions today.
However, the modest federal expenditures of the past do not capture
the full "national expenditure" during the pre-9/11 period, since airlines and airports had responsibilities with costs associated with them
that were mandated by security regulations (see Bragdon, 2008, for a
review).

In the years before the 2001 attacks, a presidential commission
had focused attention on a variety of changes it believed needed to
be made to improve the security of the aviation system. In May 1997,
in an analysis related to its review of those findings, the FAA estimated that "the total 10-year cost to the federal government, airport
authorities, and the airlines for security programs at the nation's largest
and busiest airports alone would be close to $3 billion" (GAO, 1999,
p. 5), or approximately $300 million annually. Even when adjusted
for inflation—approximately $425 million in 2011 dollars—that
estimated total is more than *15* times less than TSA's current annual
budget.[1]

Much of this increase occurred in the few years immediately following 9/11, and it appeared for a time that ever-increasing resources
would be made available to homeland security efforts. However, the
national realization of the need for broader fiscal constraints suggests
that this will not be the case going forward. Tighter budgets are drawing closer attention to the performance of aviation security invest-

---

[1]   In the Fiscal Year 2011 President's budget, the sum of the aviation security line item and
that for the Federal Air Marshal Service was approximately $6.5 billion (Office of Manage-
ment and Budget, 2011).

ments. Questions have emerged about whether our focus on threats to aircraft has led to our "overpaying" to reduce aviation security risks and neglecting other responsibilities.

Such pressures will increase the importance and potential leverage of analysis to ensure that "we get what we pay for" from aviation security programs—to ensure that investments will pay the security dividends intended and that we do not select security strategies whose costs prove to exceed our assumptions. Analysis of risks and responses to them can also help us "cut intelligently," reducing less effective efforts preferentially in pursuit of the best aggregate security performance at the least cost.

To make prudent decisions that address the real terrorist risk to aviation but also do so efficiently, we need to know the costs and the benefits of security measures. Significant progress has been made in developing analytical approaches to do so, but challenges still remain.

Cost-benefit analysis of security measures can help insulate security decisions from politics, both personal and partisan. Since criticizing security performance is a staple of partisan political debate after even unsuccessful terrorist attacks, there is a potent disincentive to scale back security in any form. Analysis also helps to provide a counterweight to individual reticence to relax security out of the entirely understandable fear on the part of decisionmakers from whatever political persuasion that doing so would let the country be attacked "on their watch."

This study explores some of the important influences and uncertainties associated with assessing and managing terrorism risk to the commercial aviation system. In so doing, we have identified a number of areas where our ability to make good decisions is hampered by a fundamental lack of understanding and information. At the same time, we have identified some ways in which, despite these knowledge gaps, we are able to develop useful insights about risks that can help guide decisionmaking. While the state of knowledge is far from being able to optimize security design and investment, our results suggest that careful consideration of available information can lead to helpful direction and improved decisionmaking.

Key Uncertainties and Knowledge Gaps

The goal of crafting truly efficient aviation security strategies is hampered by a variety of uncertainties that have been explored throughout the individual analyses in this monograph. It will always be difficult to draw clear, quantitative conclusions about terrorist preferences (threat) and security performance (vulnerability) given the evolution and adaptation by both attackers and defenders. Historical data are one window, but past performance—on both sides of the conflict—provides only some insight into likely future results. The historical record of attempted attacks on aviation systems, particularly domestically, does not provide large amounts of data on either factor. Though more intelligence information could help reduce this uncertainty, the ability of attackers to change their behavior will mean some uncertainty will always remain.

Other uncertainties affect the ability to perform detailed cost-benefit studies, including quantification of the *full costs* of attempted or successful attacks on aviation targets (most notably their indirect costs), the *full costs* of security measures (particularly more intangible effects that are difficult to value), and the *full effects* of security measures (including how they interact with one another and their effect on adversary decisionmaking and choices—feeding back to concerns about quantifying the risk to the aviation system from terrorism). These too are areas where analysis could reduce the levels of uncertainty, but only to a point—as changes in society, public preferences, and the nature of terrorist adversaries will make any estimates perishable at best.

Useful Insights Can Be Derived in Spite of Uncertainties

Though it is easy to identify uncertainties and problems that complicate analytic efforts, decisionmakers—and the policy analysts that seek to assist them—lack the option to simply conclude that those uncertainties free them of the obligation to make choices and develop security policies. As a result, our focus has been exploring ways to inform decisions *in spite of uncertainty*, rather than giving into the temptation to conclude with a plea for more data and more analysis to inform better choices sometime in the future.

Despite the great uncertainties in many areas, it is possible to draw on the tools of cost-benefit and other types of analysis to improve aviation security efforts. Though we do not have a full grasp of many intangible costs associated with aviation security efforts, our analysis shows that a break-even approach can provide useful insights into how these costs influence the net benefit of security. If the intangible costs of security translate into reduced passenger demand, the benefits of security in reducing attack risk are quickly overwhelmed by the losses stemming from the reduced value of the aviation system. Even a slight reduction in passenger demand can greatly reduce or even negate the net benefit of a security investment. This essentially raises the bar for the performance of security measures: Not only do they need to be effective in reducing the risk of attack, they must do so without sacrificing too much of the value of the system they seek to protect. Recognizing the strong influence of the indirect costs of security emphasizes the importance of designing security approaches that avoid such costs, by assembling systems of security measures that minimize the effect on passengers and other users' experience.

The conclusions of such an analysis has obvious implications for comparing different security measures—for example, our analysis of the Federal Air Marshal Service showed that its costs created a substantial bar for risk reduction to make the program cost-effective. With respect to effects on system functionality, however, the Federal Air Marshal Service compares favorably with such security measures as screening to maintain a "perimeter defense" around the system, since FAMs' effects on passenger experience (and, by extension, system utility) are much less.

Another area where our analysis reveals useful insights for security decisionmaking is understanding the merits of preferential screening proposals, such as a trusted traveler program. Despite interest in pursuing such a program, progress has been stymied because the potential benefit depends on behaviors of passengers and terrorists that are highly uncertain. Our analysis shows that even when uncertainties are great we can identify plausible conditions under which a trusted traveler program would reduce risk. Two key factors are the fraction of the traveling public that enrolls in the trusted traveler program and the fraction of terrorists that do so. Though decisionmakers cannot control these factors, they can influence them. Such insights add some clarity to a debate beset with uncertainty and ambivalence.

A final, more general area in which our analysis provides helpful insight is in the use of modeling to understand terrorism risks. The limited amount and quality of data on aviation terrorism incidents, combined with our poor understanding of terrorist behavior, makes predictive modeling of terrorism risk untenable. However, models can be designed and used for less precise and final purposes. Rather than attempting to account for all potential influences and the complex relationships among them, a simpler, low-resolution model may have just a few key parameters and allow users to develop plausible hypotheses about the conditions under which security systems might produce benefits.

Looking to the Future

In the majority of the analyses discussed here, we considered the benefit of security measures and took on various types of uncertainties that can affect how those benefits are measured and valued. Though not explicitly framed this way in all cases, the four studies that looked at the benefits of security (discussed in Chapters Four through Seven) each capture—in somewhat different ways—different complexities regarding human adaptive behavior. Though adaptation by terrorist attackers is frequently the focus in security planning, our examination of a potential trusted traveler program highlights that decisions made by passengers can have their own security implications. Irrespective of the source of the challenge, when considering a potential security investment or evaluating one that is in place now, we do not want to overstate the expected benefits, which can happen if we either neglect interactions between measures in a multilayered security system or ignore how attackers could try to use the characteristics of our security strategies to their benefit rather than our own.

Looking to the future of aviation security in the United States, the resource constraints that are almost certain to affect most policy areas will be a challenge. Such constraints will be even more difficult to navigate as the lifespan of technologies and systems used now is exhausted and decisions to recapitalize, replace, or improve them must be made over the short-, medium-, and long-term policy horizons. Major investments have been made in imaging technologies, for example, whose operational lifetime is finite—meaning that even as resources may be declining, there will be requirements to spend just to maintain the status quo, much less expand or reform the aviation security system.

For organizations and people charged with protecting citizens from harm, the potential for cuts in resources is always difficult to consider and implement. In addition to the highly charged politics surrounding homeland security measures, there will always be an understandable trepidation to make cuts out of fear that imprudent action will undermine effective security efforts. But if a sufficient analytical basis for assessing security measures and strategies is available, that trepidation can be reduced through analysis, and unavoidable resource constraints can be made into an opportunity. Constraints force choices, which in turn force evaluation to help ensure that we are not spending limited national resources in ways that are not achieving what they are intended to achieve. In aviation security, where the total cost of the national effort has expanded significantly since 9/11, such evaluation could pay dividends not just in reduced national expenditures, but also by helping to identify ways to get comparable or better security for less cost—more efficient aviation security—that could make our homeland security efforts more sustainable and make the country better off in the long run.

Bibliography

Air Transport Action Group, *The Economic and Social Benefits of Air Transport 2008*, Geneva, Switzerland: Air Transport Action Group, 2008.

Akhtar, Juned, Torkel Bjørnskau, and Knut Veisten, "Assessing Security Measures Reducing Terrorist Risk: Inverse Ex Post Cost-Benefit and Cost-Effectiveness Analyses of Norwegian Airports and Seaports," *Journal of Transportation Security*, Vol. 3, No. 3, 2010, pp. 179–195.

Aviation Safety Network, ASN Aviation Safety Database, 2012a. As of May 8, 2012:
http://aviation-safety.net/database/

———, "Contributory Cause—Security—Suicide," 2012b. As of May 31, 2012:
http://aviation-safety.net/database/dblist.php?Event=SES

Barnett, Arnold, Robert Shumsky, Mark Hansen, Amedeo Odoni, and Geoffrey Gosling, "Safe at Home? An Experiment in Domestic Airline Security," *Operations Research*, Vol. 49, No. 2, 2001, pp. 181–195.

Belcore, Jamie, and Jerry Ellig, "Homeland Security and Regulatory Analysis: Are We Safe Yet?" Mercatus Center Working Paper, 08-13, June 2008.

Bier, Vicki M., "Game-Theoretic and Reliability Methods in Counter-Terrorism and Security," in *Modern Statistical and Mathematical Methods in Reliability, Series on Quality, Reliability and Engineering Statistics*, Hackensack, N.J.: World Scientific Publishing Co., 2005.

Bier, Vicki M., Naraphorn Haphuriwat, Jaime Menoyo, Rae Zimmerman, and Alison M. Culpen, "Optimal Resource Allocation for Defense of Targets Based on Differing Measures of Attractiveness," *Risk Analysis*, Vol. 28, No. 3, 2008, pp. 763–770.

Bigelow, James H., and Paul K. Davis, *Implications for Model Validation of Multiresolution, Multiperspective Modeling (MRMPM) and Exploratory Analysis*, Santa Monica, Calif.: RAND Corporation, MR-1750-AF, 2003. As of May 3, 2012:
http://www.rand.org/pubs/monograph_reports/MR1750.html

Blakock, Garrick, Vrinda Kadiyali, and Daniel H. Simon, "Driving Fatalities After 9/11: A Hidden Cost of Terrorism," *Applied Economics*, Vol. 41, No. 14, 2009, pp. 1717–1729.

Bonner, Raymond, and Thom Shanker, "U.S. Military Officer Dies in Rocket Barrage at Baghdad Hotel," *New York Times*, October 26, 2003.

Bonomo, James, Giacomo Bergamo, David R. Frelinger, John Gordon IV, and Brian A. Jackson, *Stealing the Sword: Limiting Terrorist Use of Advanced Conventional Weapons*, MG-510-DHS, RAND Corporation, 2007. As of May 3, 2012:
http://www.rand.org/pubs/monographs/MG510.html

Borenstein, Severin, and Martin B. Zimmerman, "Market Incentives for Safe Commercial Airline Operation," *American Economic Review*, Vol. 78, No. 5, 1988, pp. 913–935.

Bosch, Jean-Claude, E. Woodrow Eckard, and Vijay Singal, "The Competitive Impact of Air Crashes: Stock Market Evidence," *Journal of Law and Economics*, Vol. 41, No. 2, 1998, pp. 503–519.

Bragdon, Clifford R., *Transportation Security*, Burlington, Mass.: Butterworth-Heinemann, 2008.

Bridger, R. S., and S. S. Freidberg, "Managers' Estimates of Safe Loads for Manual Handling: Evidence for Risk Compensation?" *Safety Science*, Vol. 32, Nos. 2–3, 1999, pp. 103–111.

Brons, Martijn, Eric Pels, Peter Nijkamp, and Piet Rietveld, "Price Elasticities of Demand for Passenger Air Travel: A Meta-Analysis," *Journal of Air Transport Management*, Vol. 8, 2002, pp. 165–175.

Brown Gerald G., Louis Anthony (Tony) Cox, Jr., "How Probabilistic Risk Assessment Can Mislead Terrorism Risk Analysts," *Risk Analysis*, Vol., 31, No. 2, 2011, pp. 196–204.

Butcher, Louise, "Aviation: Security," House of Commons Library Note, SN/BT/1246, June 14, 2011.

Cauley, Jon, and Eric Iksoon Im, "Intervention Policy Analysis of Skyjackings and Other Terrorist Incidents," *American Economic Review*, Vol. 78, No. 2, 1988, pp. 27–31.

Caulkins, Jonathan P., "CAPPS II: A Risky Choice Concerning an Untested Risk Detection Technology," *Risk Analysis*, Vol. 24, No. 4, 2004, pp. 921–924.

Cavusoglu, Huseyin, Byungwan Koh, and Srinivasan Raghunathan, "An Analysis of the Impact of Passenger Profiling for Transportation Security," *Operations Research*, Vol. 58, No. 5, 2010, pp. 1287–1302.

Chakrabarti, Samidh, and Aaron Strauss, "Carnival Booth: An Algorithm for Defeating the Computer-Aided Passenger Screening System," *First Monday*, Vol. 7, No. 10, October 2002. As of May 3, 2012:
http://firstmonday.org/htbin/cgiwrap/bin/ojs/index.php/fm/article/view/992/913

Chaturvedi, R., S. Mellema, A. Chaturvedi, M. Mulpuri, and G. Pinczuk, "Continuous Validation Framework: A Case Study of SEAS and Afghanistan," Interservice/Industry Training, Simulation, and Education Conference (I/ITSEC), 2008.

Chow, James S., James Chiesa, Paul Dreyer, Mel Eisman, Theodore W. Karasik, Joel Kvitky, Sherrill Lingel, David Ochmanek, and Chad Shirley, *Protecting Commercial Aviation Against the Shoulder-Fired Missile Threat*, Santa Monica, Calif.: RAND Corporation, OP-106-RC, 2005. As of May 3, 2012:
http://www.rand.org/pubs/occasional_papers/OP106.html

Clark, Patti, "Comment: The Impact of Security Measures on Small, Commercial Service Airports: One Perspective," *Airport Management*, Vol. 4, No. 1, October–December 2009, pp. 4–7.

Consensus Research Group, Inc., "A Study of Air Traveler Perceptions of Aviation Security Screening Procedures: Conducted for U.S. Travel Association," December 21, 2010.

Cox, Louis Anthony (Tony), Jr., "Some Limitations of "Risk = Threat × Vulnerability Consequence" for Risk Analysis of Terrorist Attacks," *Risk Analysis*, Vol. 28, No. 6, 2008, pp. 1749–1761.

———, "Improving Risk-Based Decision Making for Terrorism Applications," *Risk Analysis*, Vol. 29, No. 3, 2009, pp. 336–341.

Cragin, Kim, and Sara A. Daly, *The Dynamic Terrorist Threat: An Assessment of Group Motivations and Capabilities in a Changing World*, Santa Monica, Calif.: RAND Corporation, MR-1782-AF, 2004. As of May 3, 2012:
http://www.rand.org/pubs/monograph_reports/MR1782.html

Davidson III, Wallace N., P. R. Chandy, and Mark Cross, "Large Losses, Risk Management and Stock Returns in the Airline Industry," *Journal of Risk and Insurance*, Vol. 54, No. 1, 1987, pp. 162–172.

Davis, Paul K., "A Framework for Verification, Validation, and Accreditation," *Simulation Validation Workshop Proceedings (SIMVAL II)*, Adelia E. Ritchie, ed., Alexandria, Va.: Military Operations Research Society, 1992, Ch. VI, pp. 1–39. .

———, *Analytic Architecture for Capabilities-Based Planning, Mission-System Analysis, and Transformation*, Santa Monica, Calif.: RAND Corporation, MR-1513-OSD, 2002. As of August 15, 2007:
http://www.rand.org/pubs/monograph_reports/MR1513.html

———, "Exploratory Analysis and Implications for Modeling," in Stuart Johnson, Martin C. Libicki, and Gregory F. Treverton, eds., *New Challenges, New Tools for Defense Decisionmaking*, Santa Monica, Calif.: RAND Corporation, MR-1576-RC, 2003. As of May 3, 2012:
http://www.rand.org/pubs/monograph_reports/MR1576.html

Davis, Paul K., and Kim Cragin, eds., *Social Science for Counterterrorism: Putting the Pieces Together*, Santa Monica, Calif.: RAND Corporation, MG-849-OSD, 2009. As of May 3, 2012:
http://www.rand.org/pubs/monographs/MG849.html

Davis, Paul K., Jonathan Kulick, and Michael Egner, *Implications of Modern Decision Science for Military Decision-Support Systems*, Santa Monica, Calif.: RAND Corporation, MG-360-AF, 2005. As of May 3, 2012:
http://www.rand.org/pubs/monographs/MG360.html

Davis, Paul K., Russell D. Shaver, and Justin Beck, *Portfolio-Analysis Methods for Assessing Capability Options*, Santa Monica, Calif.: RAND Corporation, MG-662-OSD, 2008. As of May 3, 2012:
http://www.rand.org/pubs/monographs/MG662.html

Department of Defense Instruction 5000.61, *DoD Modeling and Simulation (M&S) Verification, Validation, and Accreditation (VV&A)*, Washington, D.C., December 9, 2009.

Dewar, James A., Steven C. Bankes, James S. Hodges, Thomas W. Lucas, Desmond Saunders-Newton, and Patrick Vye, *Credible Uses of the Distributed Interactive Simulation (DIS) System*, Santa Monica, Calif.: RAND Corporation, MR-607-A, 1996. As of May 3, 2012:
http://www.rand.org/pubs/monograph_reports/MR607.html

Dewar, James A., Carl H. Builder, William M. Hix, and Morlie Levin, *Assumption-Based Planning: A Planning Tool for Very Uncertain Times*, Santa Monica, Calif.: RAND Corporation, MR-1114-A, 1993. As of May 3, 2012:
http://www.rand.org/pubs/monograph_reports/MR114.html

DHS—*See* U.S. Department of Homeland Security.

Dillon, Robin L., Robert M. Liebe, and Thomas Bestafka, "Risk-Based Decision Making for Terrorism Applications," *Risk Analysis*, Vol. 29, No. 3, 2009, pp. 321–335.

Drakos, Konstantinos, and Andreas Gofas, "The Devil You Know but Are Afraid to Face: Underreporting Bias and Its Distorting Effects on the Study of Terrorism," *Journal of Conflict Resolution,* Vol. 50, No. 5, 2006, pp. 714–735.

Drury, Colin G., Kimberly M. Ghylin, and Karen Holness, "Error Analysis and Threat Magnitude for Carry-On Bag Inspection," *Proceedings of the Human Factors and Ergonomics Society 50th Annual Meeting*, 2006, pp. 1189–1193.

Eggen, Dan, "Air Attack on U.S. Consulate Foiled," *Washington Post*, May 3, 2003, p. A1.

Elias, Bart, *National Aviation Security Policy, Strategy, and Mode-Specific Plans*, RL34302, Washington, D.C.: Congressional Research Service, 2009.

———, *Airport and Aviation Security: U.S. Policy and Strategy in the Age of Global Terrorism*, Boca Raton, Fla.: CRC Press, 2010a.

———, *Screening and Securing Air Cargo: Background and Issues for Congress*, R41515, Washington, D.C.: Congressional Research Service, 2010b.

Enders, W., "Terrorism: An Empirical Analysis," in K. Hartley and T. Sandler, eds., *Handbook of Defense Economics: Defense in a Globalized World*, Vol. 2, 2007, North Holland: Amsterdam, 2007.

Enders, W., and T. Sandler, "Patterns of Transnational Terrorism, 1970–1999: Alternative Time Series Estimates," *International Studies Quarterly*, Vol. 46, 2002, pp. 145–165.

———, *The Political Economy of Terrorism*, Edinburgh: Cambridge University Press, 2006.

Ezell, Barry Charles, Steven P. Bennet, Detlof von Winterfeldt, John Sokolowski, and Andrew J. Collins, "Probabilistic Risk Analysis and Terrorism Risk," *Risk Analysis*, Vol. 30, No. 4, 2010, pp. 575–589.

FAA—*See* Federal Aviation Administration.

Fallows, James, and Jeffrey Goldberg, "TSA Chief: We Will Never Eliminate Risk," The Atlantic website, December 8, 2010. As of May 7, 2012: http://www.theatlantic.com/national/archive/2010/12/ tsa-chief-well-never-eliminate-risk/67682/1/

Federal Aviation Administration, "The Economic Impact of Civil Aviation on the U.S. Economy," October 2008.

———, "Aviation Data and Statistics, General Aviation and Part 135 Activity Surveys—CY 2009, Table 2.4—2009 General Aviation and Air Taxi Total Number of Landings by Region and Aircraft Type," last modified January 11, 2012. As of May 7, 2012: http://www.faa.gov/data_research/aviation_data_statistics/general_aviation/ CY2009/

Feng, Qianmei, "On Determining Specifications and Selections of Alternative Technologies for Airport Checked-Baggage Security Screening," *Risk Analysis*, Vol. 27, No. 5, 2007, pp. 1299–1310.

Forrest, James J. F., "The Modern Terrorist Threat to Aviation Security," *Perspectives on Terrorism*, Vol. 1, No. 6, 2008.

Freitas, Paul J., "Passenger Aviation Security, Risk Management, and Simple Physics," *Journal of Transportation Security*, Vol. 5, No. 2, 2012.

GAO—*See* U.S. Government Accountability Office or, prior to 2004, U.S. General Accounting Office.

Ghylin, K. M., C. G . Drury, and A. Schwaninger, "Two-Component Model of Security Inspection: Application and Findings," 16th World Congress of Ergonomics, IEA 2006, Maastricht, The Netherlands, July 10–14, 2006.

Gigerenzer, Gerd, "Out of the Frying Pan into the Fire: Behavioral Reactions to Terrorist Attacks," *Risk Analysis*, Vol. 26, No. 2, 2006, pp. 347–351.

Gkritza, Konstantina, Debbie Niemeier, and Fred Mannering, "Airport Security Screening and Changing Passenger Satisfaction: An Exploratory Assessment," *Journal of Air Transport Management*, Vol. 12, 2006 pp. 213–219.

Gordon, Peter, James E. Moore II, Ji Young Park, and Harry W. Richardson, "The Economic Impacts of a Terrorist Attack on the U.S. Commercial Aviation System," *Risk Analysis,* Vol. 27, No. 3, 2007, pp. 505–512.

Hartley, D. S., "Verification and Validation in Military Simulations," *Proceedings of the 1997 Winter Simulation Conference*, 1997.

Hodges, James S., "Six or So Things You Can Do with a Bad Model," *Operations Research*, Vol. 29, 1991, pp. 355–365.

Hodges, James S., and James A Dewar, *Is It You or Your Model Talking? A Framework for Model Validation*, Santa Monica, Calif.: RAND Corporation, R-4114-AF/A/OSD, 1992. As of May 31, 2012:
http://www.rand.org/pubs/reports/R4114.html

Holmes, Marcus, "Just How Much Does That Cost, Anyway? An Analysis of the Financial Costs and Benefits of the 'No-Fly' List," *Homeland Security Affairs*, Vol. 5, No. 1, 2009.

———, "National Security Behavioral Detection: A Typology of Strategies, Costs, and Benefits," *Journal of Transportation Security*, Vol. 4, No. 4, 2011, pp. 361–374.

Holt, Mark, and Anthony Andrews, "Nuclear Power Plant Security and Vulnerabilities," Washington, D.C.: Congressional Research Service, RL34331, March 18, 2009.

Hudson, A., "Air Marshals Cover Only a Few Flights," *Washington Times*, August 16, 2004.

———, "Flight Marshal Numbers Disputed, Agents Criticize Data 'Padding,'" *Washington Times*, March 3, 2005.

IATA—*See* International Air Transport Association.

International Air Transport Association, "Press Release: Short-Sighted Security Measures Hurting Airlines," 2002. As of May 3, 2012:
http://www.iata.org/pressroom/pr/Pages/2002-10-29-36.aspx

———, "Grim Prospects—Deep Recession, Bigger Losses," March 24, 2009. As of May 10, 2012:
http://www.iata.org/pressroom/pr/pages/2009-03-24-01.aspx

———, "Fact Sheet: Security," 2011. As of May 3, 2012:
http://www.iata.org/pressroom/facts_figures/fact_sheets/pages/security.aspx

Ito, Harumi, and Darin Lee, "Assessing the Impact of the September 11 Terrorist Attacks on U.S. Airline Demand," *Journal of Economics and Business*, Vol. 57, No. 1, 2005, pp. 75–95.

Jackson, Brian A., "Exploring the Utility of Considering Cost-Effectiveness Analysis of Domestic Intelligence Policy Change," in Brian A. Jackson, ed., *The Challenge of Domestic Intelligence in a Free Society: A Multidisciplinary Look at the Creation of a U.S. Domestic Counterterrorism Intelligence Agency*, Santa Monica, Calif.: RAND Corporation, MG-804-DHS, 2009a. As of May 3, 2012:
http://www.rand.org/pubs/monographs/MG804.html

———, "Technology Strategies for Homeland Security: Adaptation and Coevolution of Offense and Defense," *Homeland Security Affairs*, Vol. 5, No. 1, 2009b.

Jackson, Brian A., John C. Baker, Peter Chalk, Kim Cragin, John V. Parachini, and Horacio R. Trujillo, *Aptitude for Destruction*, Volume 1: *Organizational Learning in Terrorist Groups and Its Implications for Combating Terrorism*, Santa Monica, Calif.: RAND Corporation, MG-331-NIJ, 2005a. As of May 3, 2012:
http://www.rand.org/pubs/monographs/MG331.html

———, *Aptitude for Destruction*, Volume 2: *Case Studies of Organizational Learning in Five Terrorist Groups*, Santa Monica, Calif.: RAND Corporation, MG-332-NIJ, 2005b. As of May 3, 2012:
http://www.rand.org/pubs/monographs/MG332.html

Jackson Brian A., Peter Chalk, Kim Cragin, Bruce Newsome, John V. Parachini, William Rosenau, Erin M. Simpson, Melanie W. Sisson, and Donald Temple, *Breaching the Fortress Wall: Understanding Terrorist Efforts to Overcome Defensive Technologies*, Santa Monica, Calif.: RAND Corporation, MG-481-DHS, 2007. As of May 3, 2012:
http://www.rand.org/pubs/monographs/MG481.html

Jackson, Brian A., Edward W. Chan, and Tom LaTourrette, "Assessing the Security Benefits of a Trusted Traveler Program in the Presence of Attempted Attacker Exploitation and Compromise," *Journal of Transportation Security*, Vol. 5, No. 1, 2012, pp. 1–34.

Jackson, Brian A., Lloyd Dixon, and Victoria A. Greenfield, *Economically Targeted Terrorism: A Review of the Literature and a Framework for Considering Defensive Approaches*, Santa Monica, Calif.: RAND Corporation, TR-476-CTRMP, 2007. As of May 3, 2012:
http://www.rand.org/pubs/technical_reports/TR476.html

Jackson, Brian A., and David R. Frelinger, *Emerging Threats and Security Planning: How Should We Decide What Hypothetical Threats to Worry About?* Santa Monica, Calif.: RAND Corporation, OP-256-RC, 2009. As of May 3, 2012: http://www.rand.org/pubs/occasional_papers/OP256.html

Jacobson, Sheldon H., Tamana Karnani, and John E. Kobza, "Assessing the Impact of Deterrence on Aviation Checked Baggage Screening Strategies," *International Journal of Risk Assessment & Management*, Vol. 5, No. 1, 2005, pp. 1–15.

Jacobson, Sheldon H., Julie L. Virta, Jon M. Bowman, John E. Kobza, and John J. Nestor, "Modeling Aviation Baggage Screening Security Systems: A Case Study," *IIE Transactions*, Vol. 35, 2003, pp. 259–269.

Jenkins, Brian Michael, *The Terrorist Threat to Commercial Aviation*, Santa Monica, Calif.: RAND Corporation, P-7540, 1989. As of May 3, 2012: http://www.rand.org/pubs/papers/P7540.html

Johnston, Roger G., "Lessons for Layering," *Security Management*, January 2010, pp. 65–68.

Johnston, Van R., "Terrorism and Transportation Policy and Administration: Balancing the Model and Equations for Optimal Security," *Review of Policy Research*, Vol. 21, No. 3, 2004, pp. 263–274.

Johnstone, R. William, *9/11 and the Future of Transportation Security*, Westport, Conn.: Praeger Security International, 2006.

Jones, Charisse, "For Some, Hassles Dim the Appeal of Air Travel," *USA Today*, January 12, 2010.

Jones, Roderick, "Hack-Jet: Losing a Commercial Airliner in a Networked World," Counterterrorismblog.org, June 9, 2009.

Jorgensen, F., and P. A. Pedersen, "Drivers' Response to the Installation of Road Lighting: An Economic Interpretation," *Accident Analysis and Prevention,* Vol. 34, No. 5, 2002, pp. 601–608.

Jung, J. M., and E. T. Fujii, "The Price Elasticity of Demand for Air Travel: Some New Evidence," *Journal of Transport Economics and Policy*, Vol. 10, No. 3, September 1976, pp. 257–262.

Kakalik, James S., Elizabeth M. King, Michael Traynor, Patricia A. Ebener, and Larry Pincus, *Costs and Compensation Paid in Aviation Accident Litigation*, Santa Monica, Calif.: RAND Corporation, R-3421-CJ, 1988. As of May 3, 2012: http://www.rand.org/pubs/reports/R3421.html

Kaufman, Leon, and Joseph W. Carlson, "An Evaluation of Airport X-Ray Backscatter Units Based on Image Characteristics," *Journal of Transportation Security*, Vol. 4, No. 1, 2010, pp. 73–94.

Kaufmann, Daniel, "Revamping Aviation Security: Think Outside of the Terminal," Brookings Institution Up Front Blog, December 5, 2010. As of May 3, 2012:
http://www.brookings.edu/opinions/2010/0210_aviation_security_kaufmann.aspx

Keeney Gregory L., and Detlof von Winterfeldt, "Identifying and Structuring the Objectives of Terrorists," *Risk Analysis*, Vol. 30, No. 12, 2010, pp. 1803–1816.

Keeney, Ralph L., "Modeling Values for Anti-Terrorism Analysis," *Risk Analysis*, Vol. 27, No. 3, 2007, pp. 585–596.

Kenney, Michael, *From Pablo to Osama: Trafficking and Terrorist Networks, Government Bureaucracies, and Competitive Adaptation*, University Park, Pa.: Pennsylvania State University Press, 2006.

King, Elizabeth M., and James P. Smith, *Economic Loss and Compensation in Aviation Accidents*, Santa Monica, Calif.: RAND Corporation, R-3551-ICJ, 1988. As of May 3, 2012:
http://www.rand.org/pubs/reports/R3551.html

Kobza, John E., and Sheldon H. Jacobson, "Addressing the Dependency Problem in Access Security System Architecture Design," *Risk Analysis*, Vol. 16, No. 6, 1996, pp. 801–812.

———, "Probability Models for Access Security System Architectures," *Journal of the Operational Research Society*, Vol. 48, No. 3, 1997, pp. 255–263.

Koopman, B. O., "The Theory of Search, II: Target Detection," *Operations Research*, Vol. 4, No. 5, 1956, pp. 503–531.

Krause, Kent C., "Putting the Transportation Security Administration in Historical Context," *Journal of Air Law and Commerce*, Vol. 68, 2003, pp. 233–251.

Lempert, Robert J., Steven W. Popper, and Steven C. Bankes, *Shaping the Next One Hundred Years: New Methods for Quantitative Long-Term Policy Analysis*, Santa Monica, Calif.: RAND Corporation, MR-1626-RPC, 2003. As of May 3, 2012:
http://www.rand.org/pubs/monograph_reports/MR1626.html

Lempert, Robert J., and Michael E. Schlesinger, "Robust Strategies for Abating Climate Change," *Climatic Change*, Vol. 45, 2000, pp. 387–401.

Leone, Kelly, and Rongfang (Rachel) Liu, "The Key Design Parameters of Checked Baggage Security Screening Systems in Airports," *Journal of Air Transport Management*, Vol. 11, 2005, pp. 69–78.

Loidolt, Bryce, "Managing the Global and Local: The Dual Agendas of Al Qaeda in the Arabian Peninsula," *Studies in Conflict and Terrorism*, Vol. 34, No. 2., 2011, pp. 102–123.

Lord, Steven, Rick Nunes-Vaz, Alexei Filinkov, and Glenis Crane, "Airport Front-of-House Vulnerabilities and Mitigation Options," *Journal of Transportation Security*, Vol. 3, No. 3, 2010, pp. 149–177.

Lowenthal, Micah D., testimony before the Committee on Homeland Security and Governmental Affairs, U.S. Senate, hearing on "Nuclear Terrorism: Strengthening our Domestic Defenses," June 30, 2010.

Martonosi, Susan E., and Arnold Barnett, "How Effective Is Security Screening of Airline Passengers?" *Interfaces*, Vol. 36, No. 6, 2006, pp. 545–552.

Masse, Todd, Siobhan O'Neil, and John Rollins, *The Department of Homeland Security's Risk Assessment Methodology: Evolution, Issues and Options for Congress*, Washington, D.C.: Congressional Research Service, February 2, 2007.

Maxon, Terry, "Going the Distance: Cost, Time Has Shorter Hauls Falling out of Favor with Airline Passengers," *Dallas Morning News*, January 13, 2011.

McCormick, G. H., "Terrorist Decision Making," *Annual Review of Political Science*, Vol. 6, No. 1, 2003, pp. 473–507.

McLay Laura A., Sheldon H. Jacobson, and John E. Kobza, "Making Skies Safer: Applying Analytics to Aviation Passenger Prescreening Systems," *Analytics*, Spring 2008, pp. 12–17.

McLay, Laura A., Adrian J. Lee, and Sheldon H. Jacobson, "Risk-Based Policies for Airport Security Checkpoint Screening," *Transportation Science*, Vol. 44, No. 3, 2010, pp. 333–349.

Meckler, Laura, and Sudan Carey, "Sky Patrol: U.S. Air Marshal Service Navigates Turbulent Times," *Wall Street Journal*, February 9, 2007.

Meeks, Brock N., "For Air Marshals, Less Equals More," MSNBC, September 15, 2004.

Miljkovic, Dragan, William Nganje, and Benjamin Onyango, "Offsetting Behavior and the Benefits of Food Safety Regulation," *Journal of Food Safety*, Vol. 29, 2009, pp. 49–58.

Morral, Andrew R., and Brian A. Jackson, *Understanding the Role of Deterrence in Counterterrorism Security*, Santa Monica, Calif.: RAND Corporation, OP-281-RC, 2009. As of May 3, 2012:
http://www.rand.org/pubs/occasional_papers/OP281

Morral, Andrew, Carter Price, David Ortiz, Brad Wilson, Tom LaTourrette, Blake W. Mobley, Shawn Mckay, and Henry Willis, *Modeling Terrorism Risk to the Air Transportation System: An Independent Assessment of TSA's Risk Management Assessment Tool and Associated Methods*, Santa Monica, Calif.: RAND Corporation, forthcoming.

Mueller, J., "Harbinger or Aberration: A 9/11 Provocation," *National Interest*, Fall 2002, pp. 45–50.

Mueller, J. E., and M. G. Stewart, "A Risk and Cost-Benefit Assessment of United States Aviation Security Measures," *Journal of Transportation Security*, Vol. 1, 2008, pp. 143–159.

———, *Terror, Security, and Money: Balancing the Risks, Benefits, and Costs of Homeland Security*, Oxford University Press, 2011.

National Academies, *Defending the U.S. Air Transportation System Against Chemical and Biological Threats*, Washington, D.C.: National Academies Press, 2006.

———, *Protecting Individual Privacy in the Struggle Against Terrorists: A Framework for Program Assessment*, Washington, D.C.: National Academies Press, 2008a.

National Research Council, *Review of the Department of Homeland Security's Approach to Risk Analysis*, Washington, D.C.: National Academies Press, 2010.

National Research Council, Committee on Commercial Aviation Security, *Airline Passenger Security Screening: New Technology and Implementation Issues*, Washington, D.C.: National Academies Press, 1996.

National Research Council, Committee on Methodological Improvements to the Department of Homeland Security's Biological Agent Risk Analysis, *Department of Homeland Security Bioterrorism Risk Assessment: A Call for Change*, Washington, D.C.: National Academies Press, 2008b.

National Research Council, Panel on Assessment of Technologies Deployed to Improve Aviation Security, *Assessment of Technologies Deployed to Improve Aviation Security: First Report*, Washington, D.C.: National Academies Press, 1999.

Nganje, William, Dragan Miljkovic, and Elvis Ndembe, "Offsetting Behavior and the Benefits of Food Safety Policies in Vegetable Preparation and Consumption," *Agribusiness*, Vol. 26, No. 4, 2010, pp. 557–572.

Office of Management and Budget, *Budget of the United States Government, Fiscal Year 2010*, Washington, D.C., 2010.

———, *Budget of the United States Government, Fiscal Year 2011: Appendix*, Washington, D.C., 2011.

OMB—*See* Office of Management and Budget.

Oster, Clinton V., and John S. Strong, "An Assessment of Aviation Security Costs and Funding in the United States," in Andrew R. Thomas, ed., *Aviation Security Management*, Volume 3, *Perspectives on Aviation Security Management*, Westport, Conn.: Praeger Security International, 2008.

Oum, Tae Hoon, W. G. Waters II, and Jong-Say Yong, "Concepts of Price Elasticities of Transport Demand and Recent Empirical Estimates: An Interpretative Survey," *Journal of Transport Economics and Policy*, Vol. 26, No. 2, May 1992, pp. 139–154.

Pace, Dale K., "Modeling and Simulation Verification and Validation Challenges," *Johns Hopkins APL Technical Digest*, Vol. 25, No. 2, 2004, pp 163–172.

Pacheco, Leticia J., John E. Kobza, Sheldon H. Jacobson, and Rajat Gupta, "A Markov Model of Terrorist Behavior Within the Aviation Security Environment," *Journal of Transportation Security*, Vol. 4, No. 2, 2011, pp. 117–130.

Parnell, Gregory S., Christopher M. Smith, and Frederick I. Moxley, "Intelligent Adversary Risk Analysis: A Bioterrorism Risk Management Model, *Risk Analysis*, Vol. 30, No. 1, 2010, pp. 32–48.

Peltzman, Sam, "The Effects of Automobile Safety Regulation," *Journal of Political Economy*, Vol. 83, 1975, pp. 677–725.

Persico, Nicola, and Petra E. Todd, "Passenger Profiling, Imperfect Screening, and Airport Security," *American Economic Review*, Vol. 95, No. 2, May 2005, pp. 127–131.

Peterson, Robert M., Raymond H. Bittel, Christopher A. Forgie, William H. Lee, and John J. Nestor, "Using USCAP's Analytical Models, the Transportation Security Administration Balances the Impacts of Aviation Security Policies on Passengers and Airlines," *Interfaces*, Vol. 37, No. 1, 2007, pp. 52–67.

Pitzer, C., "The New Management of Risk: Competency-Based Safety," *Ninth AusIMM Underground Operators Conference 2005*, Australasian Institute of Mining and Metallurgy Publication Series, 2005, pp. 395–400.

Poole, Robert W., Jr., *Airport Security: Time for a New Model*, Policy Study 340, Reason Foundation, 2006.

Poole, Robert W., Jr., and George Passantino, *A Risk-Based Airport Security Policy*, Policy Study 308, Reason Foundation, 2003.

The Port Authority of New York and New Jersey, "PA Proposes Record Level of Security Investments for 2006; Bistate Agency's Security Costs This Decade Approach $3 Billion," press release, October 20, 2005. As of May 10, 2012: http://www.panynj.gov/press-room/press-item.cfm?headLine_id=682

Press, William, "To Catch a Terrorist: Can Ethnic Profiling Work?" *Significance*, December 2010, pp. 164–167.

Rabasa, Angel, Robert D. Blackwill, Peter Chalk, Kim Cragin, C. Christine Fair, Brian A. Jackson, Brian Michael Jenkins, Seth G. Jones, Nathaniel Shestak, and Ashley J. Tellis, *The Lessons of Mumbai*, Santa Monica, Calif.: RAND Corporation, OP-249-RC, 2009. As of May 3, 2012: http://www.rand.org/pubs/occasional_papers/OP249.html

Reddick, Sharron R., "Point: The Case for Profiling," *International Social Science Review*, Vol. 79, Nos. 3–4, 2011, pp. 154–156.

Research and Innovative Technology Administration, Bureau of Transportation Statistics, "Airlines and Airports," 2011a. As of May 3, 2012: http://www.bts.gov/programs/airline_information/

———, "Glossary," 2011b. As of May 3, 2012: http://www.transtats.bts.gov/Glossary.asp

RITA—*See* Research and Innovative Technology Administration, Bureau of Transportation Statistics.

Ritchie, Adelia E., ed., *Simulation Validation Workshop Proceedings (SIMVAL II)*, Alexandria, Va.: MORS, 1992.

Robinson, Lisa A., James K. Hammitt, Joseph E. Aldy, Alan Krupnick, and Jennifer Baxter, "Valuing the Risk of Death from Terrorist Attacks," *Journal of Homeland Security and Emergency Management*, Vol. 7, No. 1, 2010, p. 14.

Rossiter, Adrianam, and Martin Dresner, "The Impact of the September 11th Security Fee and Passenger Wait Time on Traffic Diversion and Highway Fatalities," *Journal of Air Transport Management*, Vol. 10, 2004, pp. 227–232.

Sagan, Scott D., "The Problem of Redundancy Problem: Why More Nuclear Security Forces May Produce Less Nuclear Security," *Risk Analysis*, Vol. 24, No. 4, 2004, pp. 935–946.

Sargent, Robert G., "Validation and Verification of Simulation Models," in M. E. Kuhl, N. M. Steiger, F. B. Armstrong, and J. A. Joines, eds., *Proceedings of the 2005 Winter Simulation Conference*, 2005, pp. 130–143.

Saxton, Jim, "Economic Perspectives on Terrorism Insurance," Joint Economic Committee, U.S. Congress, May 2002.

Schroer, Gregory Robert, "Doomed to Repeat the Past: How the TSA Is Picking Up Where the FAA Left Off," *Transportation Law Journal*, Vol. 32, 2004, pp. 73–93.

Schwartz, Peter, *The Art of the Long View*, New York: Doubleday, 1996.

Seidenstat, Paul, "Terrorism, Airport Security, and the Private Sector," *Review of Policy Research*, Vol. 21, No. 3, 2004, pp. 275–291.

Seitz, R., "Weaker Than We Think," *American Conservative*, Vol. 6, 2004.

Slaughter, Richard, *The Knowledge Base of Futures Studies*, 2005.

Sobel, Russell S., and Todd M. Nesbit, "Automobile Safety Regulation and the Incentive to Drive Recklessly: Evidence from NASCAR," *Southern Economic Journal*, Vol. 74, No. 1, 2007, pp. 71–84.

Srinivasan, Sivaramakrishnan, Chandra R. Bhat, and Jose Holguin-Veras, "Empirical Analysis of the Impact of Security Perception on Intercity Mode Choice: A Panel Rank-Ordered Mixed-Logit Model," *Transportation Research Record*, Vol. 1942, 2006, pp. 9–15.

Stewart, Mark G., "Risk-Informed Decision Support for Assessing the Costs and Benefits of Counter-Terrorism Protective Measures for Infrastructure," *International Journal of Critical Infrastructure Protection*, Vol. 3, 2010, pp. 29–40.

Stewart, Mark G., and John Mueller, "A Risk and Cost-Benefit Assessment of United States Aviation Security Measures," *Journal of Transportation Security*, Vol. 1, No. 3, 2008, pp. 143–159.

———, "Cost-Benefit Analysis of Advanced Imaging Technology Full Body Scanners for Airline Passenger Security Screening," *Journal of Homeland Security and Emergency Management*, Vol. 8, No. 1, 2011, Article 30.

Su, Jenny C., Alisia G. T. T. Tran, John G. Wirtz, Rita A. Langteau, and Alexander J. Rothman, "Driving Under the Influence (of Stress): Evidence of a Regional Increase in Impaired Driving and Traffic Fatalities After the September 11 Terrorist Attacks," *Psychological Science*, Vol. 20, No. 1, 2009, pp. 59–65.

Thomas, Andrew R., ed., *Aviation Security Management,* Volumes 1–3, Westport, Conn.: Praeger Security International, 2008.

Thompson Jr., W. C., *One Year Later: The Fiscal Impact of 9/11 on New York City*, New York: City of New York Office of the Comptroller, September 4, 2002.

Transportation Security Administration, "How It Works: Risk Based Security Initiative," no date-a. As of May 3, 2012:
http://www.tsa.gov/what_we_do/howitworks.shtm

———, "Layers of Security: What We Do," no date-b. As of May 11, 2012:
http://www.tsa.gov/what_we_do/layers/index.shtm

U.S. Department of Homeland Security, *FY 2011 Budget in Brief,* no date. As of May 3, 2012:
http://www.dhs.gov/xlibrary/assets/budget_bib_fy2011.pdf

———, FY2012 Congressional Budget Justification, Department of Homeland Security, Washington, D.C., 2010.

U.S. Department of Homeland Security, Office of Inspector General, *TSA's Role in General Aviation Security*, OIG-09-69, May 2009.

———, *Evaluation of Newly Deployed and Enhanced Technology and Practices at the Passenger Screening Checkpoint (Unclassified Summary)*, OIG-10-75, March 2010.

U.S. General Accounting Office, *Aviation Security: FAA's Actions to Study Responsibilities and Funding for Airport Security and to Certify Screening Companies*, Washington, D.C., GAO/RCED-99-53, February 1999.

———, *Aviation Security: Registered Traveler Program Policy and Implementation Issues*, Washington, D.C., GAO-03-253, 2002a.

———, *Review of Studies of the Economic Impact of the September 11, 2001, Terrorist Attacks on the World Trade Center*, GAO-02-700R, Washington, D.C., 2002b.

U.S. Government Accountability Office, *Aviation Security: Federal Action Needed to Strengthen Domestic Air Cargo Security*, GAO-06-76, Washington, D.C., October 17, 2005.

———, *Aviation Security: Risk, Experience, and Customer Concerns Drive Changes to Airline Passenger Screening Procedures, but Evaluation and Documentation of Proposed Changes Could Be Improved*, GAO-07-634, Washington, D.C., April 16, 2007a.

———, *Aviation Security: Cost Estimates Related to TSA Funding of Checked Baggage Screening Systems at Los Angeles and Ontario Airports*, GAO-07-445, Washington, D.C., 2007b.

———, *Transportation Security: TSA Has Developed a Risk-Based Covert Testing Program, but Could Better Mitigate Aviation Security Vulnerabilities Identified Through Covert Tests*, GAO-08-958, Washington, D.C., August 8, 2008a.

———, *Transportation Security: Efforts to Strengthen Aviation and Surface Transportation Security Continue to Progress, but More Work Remains*, GAO-08-651T, Washington, D.C., April 15, 2008b.

———, *Transportation Security: Comprehensive Risk Assessments and Stronger Internal Controls Needed to Help Inform TSA Resource Allocation*, Washington D.C., GAO-09-492, March 2009a. As of May 3, 2012: http://www.gao.gov/new.items/d09492.pdf

———, *Aviation Security: A National Strategy and Other Actions Would Strengthen TSA's Efforts to Secure Commercial Airport Perimeters and Access Controls*, GAO-09-399, Washington, D.C., September 30, 2009b.

———, *Aviation Security: DHS and TSA Have Researched, Developed, and Begun Deploying Passenger Checkpoint Screening Technologies, but Continue to Face Challenges*, GAO-10-128, Washington, D.C., October 7, 2009c.

———, *Aviation Security: TSA Is Increasing Procurement and Deployment of the Advanced Imaging Technology, but Challenges to This Effort and Other Areas of Aviation Security Remain*, GAO-10-484T, Washington, D.C., March 17, 2010.

———, *General Aviation: Security Assessments at Selected Airports*, GAO-11-298, Washington, D.C., May 2011.

U.S. House of Representatives, Committee on Homeland Security, Subcommittee on Economic Security, Infrastructure Protection, and Cyber Security, "The Promise of Registered Traveler: Part I and II," 109th Congress, First Session, Washington, D.C., June 9 and June 16, 2005.

U.S. House of Representatives, Committee on Homeland Security, Subcommittee on Management, Investigations and Oversight, *Protecting the Protectors: Examining the Personnel Challenges Facing the Federal Air Marshal Service*, 111th Congress, First Session, Washington, D.C., July 23, 2009a.

U.S. House of Representatives, Committee on Homeland Security, Subcommittee on Transportation Security and Infrastructure Protection, *General Aviation Security: Assessing Risks and the Road Ahead*, 111th Congress, First Session, Washington, D.C., July 15, 2009b.

U.S. House of Representatives, Committee on Homeland Security, Subcommittee on Transportation Security and Infrastructure Protection, *The Future of the Registered Traveler Program*, 111th Congress, First Session, Washington, D.C., September 30, 2009c.

U.S. House of Representatives, Committee on Homeland Security, Subcommittee on Transportation Security and Infrastructure Protection, *100 Percent Air Cargo Screening: Remaining Steps to Secure Passenger Aircraft*, 111th Congress, Second Session, Washington, D.C., June 30, 2010a.

U.S. House of Representatives, Committee on Homeland Security, Subcommittee on Transportation Security and Infrastructure Protection, *Assessment of Checkpoint Security: Are Our Airports Keeping Passengers Safe?* 111th Congress: Second Session, Washington, D.C., March 17, 2010b.

U.S. House of Representatives, Committee on Transportation and Infrastructure, Subcommittee on Aviation, "Lasers: A Hazard to Aviation Safety and Security," Hearing, 109th Congress, First Session, Washington, D.C., March 15, 2005.

U.S. House of Representatives, Committee on Transportation and Infrastructure, Subcommittee on Aviation, *Aviation Security: An Update*, 110th Congress, Second Session, Washington, D.C., July 24, 2008.

U.S. Senate, Committee on Commerce, Science, and Transportation, *The State of Aviation Security: Is Our Current System Capable of Meeting the Threat?* 111th Congress, Second Session, January 20, 2010.

Viscusi, W. Kip, "The Lulling Effect: The Impact of Child-Resistant Packaging on Aspirin and Analgesic Ingestions," *American Economic Review*, Vol. 74, No. 2, May 1984, pp. 324–327.

Visiongain, "The Aviation Security Market, 2001–2021: Report Details," 2011. As of May 3, 2012: http://www.visiongain.com/Report/589/The-Aviation-Security-Market-2011-2021

von Bastian, C. C., A. Schwaninger, and S. Michel, "Do Multi-View X-Ray Systems Improve X-Ray Image Interpretation in Airport Security Screening?" *Zeitschrift für Arbeitswissenschaft*, Vol. 3, 2008, pp. 166–173.

von Winterfeldt, D., and T. M. O'Sullivan, "Should We Protect Commercial Airplanes Against Surface-to-Air Missile Attacks by Terrorists?" *Decision Analysis*, Vol. 3, 2006, pp. 63–75.

Weikel, Dan, "Councilwoman Calls for Audit of LAX Security," *Los Angeles Times*, August 5, 2010.

White House Commission on Aviation Safety and Security ("the Gore Commission"), *Final Report to President Clinton*, February 12, 1997.

Wilde, Gerald J. S., *Target Risk 2: A New Psychology of Safety and Health,* PDE Publications, 2001.

Wilkinson, Paul, and Brian M. Jenkins, *Aviation Terrorism and Security*, London, UK: Frank Cass, 1999.

Willis, Henry H., and Tom LaTourrette, "Using Probabilistic Terrorism Risk Modeling for Regulatory Benefit-Cost Analysis: Application to the Western Hemisphere Travel Initiative in the Land Environment," *Risk Analysis*, Vol. 28, No. 2, 2008, pp. 325–339.

Willis, Henry H., Andrew R. Morral, Terrence K. Kelly, and Jamison Jo Medby, *Estimating Terrorism Risk*, Santa Monica, Calif.: RAND Corporation, MG-388-RC, 2005. As of May 3, 2012:
http://www.rand.org/pubs/monographs/MG388.html

Wilson, Jeremy M., Brian A. Jackson, Mel Eisman, Paul Steinberg, and K. Jack Riley, *Securing America's Passenger-Rail Systems*, Santa Monica, Calif.: RAND Corporation, MG-705-NIJ, 2007. As of May 3, 2012:
http://www.rand.org/pubs/monographs/MG705.html

Yellman, Ted W., "Redundancy in Designs," *Risk Analysis*, Vol. 26, No. 1, 2006, pp. 277–286.

Yetman, James, "Suicidal Terrorism and Discriminatory Screening: An Efficiency-Equity Trade-Off," *Defence and Peace Economics*, Vol. 15, No. 3, 2004, pp. 221–230.

Figure S.1
Projected Working-Age Populations (in millions) of 15 Large Countries Under Medium Variant and Constant-Fertility Variant Projections

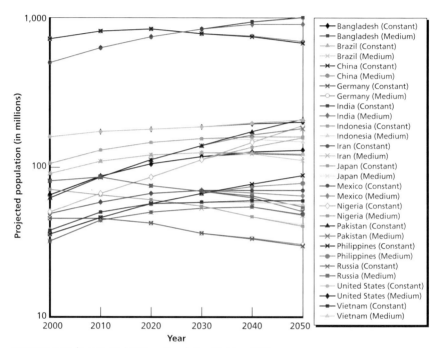

SOURCE: Data from United Nations Population Division, 2009.
RAND *MG1091-S.1*

Europe's Muslim population resemble those of the countries from which it draws its immigrants, then the Muslim share of France's and Germany's working-age populations reaches roughly 15 and 10 percent, respectively, by 2050. By contrast, Russia's Muslim population could double to reach 30 percent of the total.

Incomes

To the extent that a nation's power depends on its gross domestic product (GDP), it is possible that large, putatively unpredictable differences in economic growth rates from one country to another could swamp the slow but predictable international differences in population growth rates. If so, population may be quite secondary in evaluating a nation's potential military power.

To determine whether this might be so, the research reported here looked backward at the rate of change in national per capita GDP from 1980 to 2007 for the 37 most populous countries.[1] The numbers indicate that the standard deviation in annual per capita GDP growth rates (1.94 percent) is only 50 percent larger than the prospective standard deviation in the growth of working-age populations from 2010 to 2030 (on average, 1.29 percent). If China and Congo are excluded, the two numbers are closer: 1.46 percent for GDP per capita and 1.24 percent for prospective working-age populations. Although international economic growth variations are larger, they are not overwhelmingly so. Demographic change can be regarded as a separate and important influence on a nation's power. Because the per capita GDP growth of rich countries has been roughly the same since 1980, demographic growth assumes singular importance in making international comparisons among them.

However, past income growth and future population growth (which is to say, past birthrates) are negatively correlated to a modest extent: Every 1-percent difference in the former is associated with a 0.25-percent difference in the latter.

Aging

Nearly every country in the world (and the rural areas of all countries) is aging, and the number of people above working age will rise relative to the number of working-age adults. Today, Brazil has 18 older individuals for every 100 working-age adults; Japan, 53. Accounting for population aging, projections indicate that by 2050 Brazil will have 59 older individuals for every 100 working-age adults; Japan, today and in the future among the most aged countries in the world, will have 109

---

[1]   GDP is measured in purchasing power parity, as measured by the World Bank (World Databank, "World Development Indicators, 2007," accessed December 15, 2010), divided by the working-age population.

The next three graphs illustrate total fertility rates for the world's 55 largest countries (ranked in terms of their projected 2020 population) divided into three groups: upper-, middle-, and lower-income (based on current per capita incomes as measured by the World Bank[6]).

Figure 2.1 depicts ten large rich countries. All of them had, by today's standards, moderately high fertility rates through the early 1960s (South Korea's rate was significantly higher, but it was a poor country then).[7] By the late 1970s, all but two of them—Spain and South Korea, neither rich at that point—were below ZPG. The U.S. fertility rate bottomed out in the late 1970s and has returned to ZPG level; its fertility rate leads that of the larger rich nations. Every other nation is still below ZPG. One can see some recovery in fertility rates over the last ten or so years. This may represent a slight change in attitudes or decisions by women in their 30s and early 40s to finally have the children they had earlier postponed. Yet, one should not exaggerate the impact of changes in birth timing on fertility rates; Appendix A demonstrates that the effects can be small and temporary. Because rich states have been below ZPG for well over a generation, the size of their child-bearing cohort has been correspondingly reduced, which means that even a return to relatively high fertility rates is unlikely to restore native (i.e., nonimmigrant) population levels anytime soon.

Figure 2.2 depicts the course of fertility for middle-income countries. Although the trends for each country are similar, there are disparities among countries, in large part because today's middle-income countries have been on different development paths. Until 1975, for

---

[6] Eric Swanson, *World Development Indicators 2007*, Washington, D.C.: World Bank, April 1, 2004.

[7] Billari, Kohler, and Myrskyla argue that recent rises in fertility are more than random (or represent babies finally born to women who have postponed childrearing). They point to a systematic positive correlation between a country's fertility levels and its human development index (HDI) once the index crosses a particular level (represented, roughly put, by Eastern Europe). Although their thesis may be proven correct in time, such conclusions may be premature. The number of countries with high HDIs is small, the data points are clumpy (five of the high-HDI countries are Scandinavian and, for that reason, may be expected to be similar), and there are important exceptions (e.g., Japan, Canada) (Francesco Billari, Hans-Peter Kohler, and Mikko Myrskyla, "Advances in Development Reverse Fertility Decline," *Nature,* August 6, 2009, pp. 741–743).

Figure 2.1
Total Fertility Rate Trends by Country—Upper-Income Countries

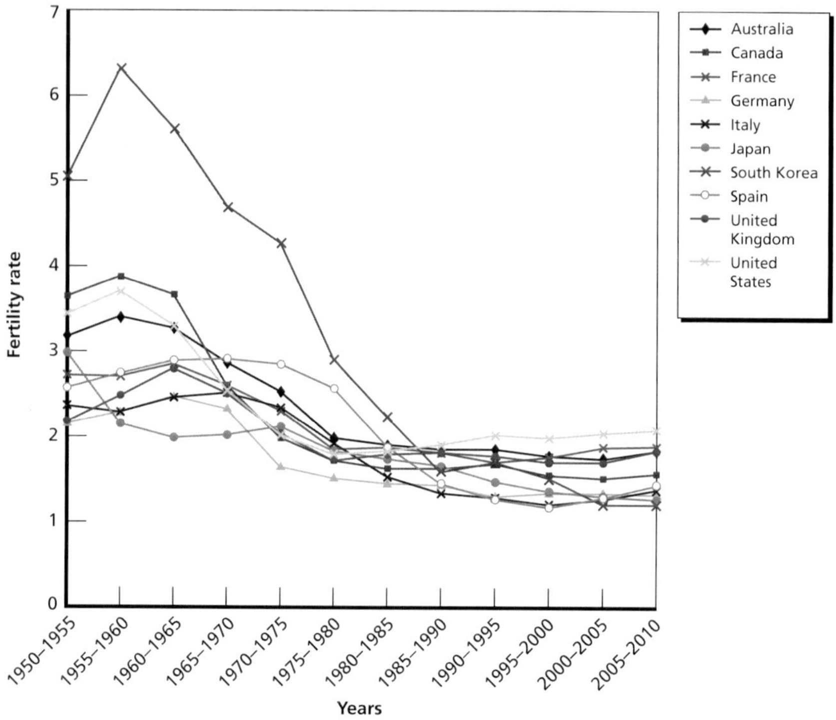

SOURCE: Data from United Nations Population Division, 2009.
RAND MG1091-2.1

instance, four medium-fertility-rate countries, Poland, Argentina, Russia, and Ukraine (all at least partially industrialized prior to World War II), stood in high contrast to the 19 high-fertility-rate countries, all of whom had a total fertility rate over 4.5, and some of which were as high as 7.5. Russia, Poland, and Ukraine, in particular, now have very low fertility rates and rapidly aging populations. Starting in the mid-1970s, a substantial decline among China and the other 18 countries set in. The three core Arab countries in the mix, Syria, Iraq, and Saudi Arabia, were late into the fertility decline (Algeria, Egypt, and Iran were almost as late) and, as a consequence, still have rather high fertility levels. Other than those three, the highest fertility rate among middle-income countries is 3.1 (the Philippines), and many middle-

Figure 2.2
Total Fertility Rate Trends by Country—Middle-Income Countries

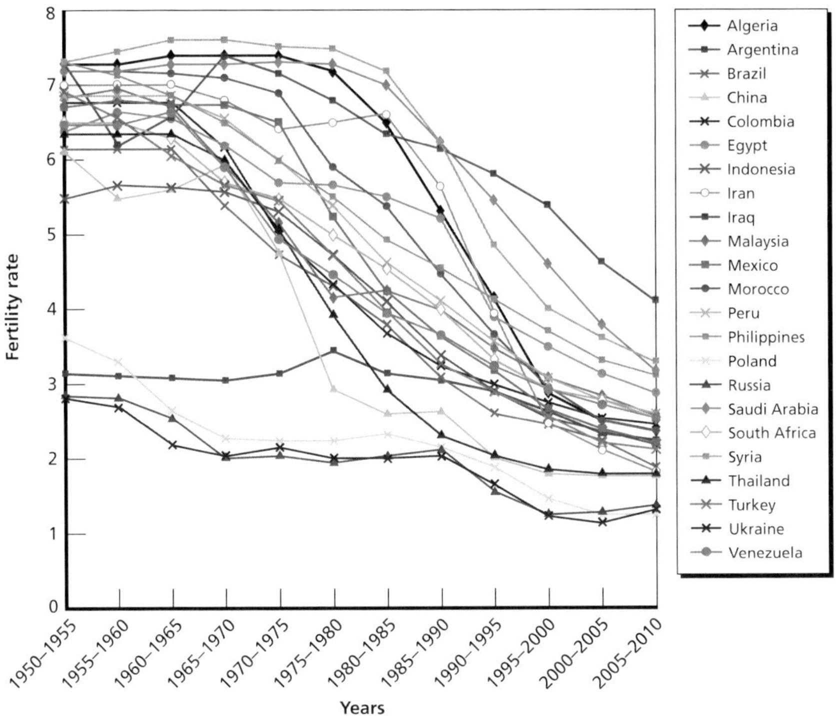

SOURCE: Data from United Nations Population Division, 2009.
RAND *MG1091-2.2*

income countries (the four long-industrialized nations, plus China, Brazil, Thailand, and Iran) have fertility rates below ZPG levels.

Figure 2.3 depicts lower-income countries. Here, the clustering patterns are different. With the exception of North Korea (semi-industrialized by the end of World War II), all of the large poor countries had fertility rates in excess of five children per woman through the mid-1970s—indeed, on the whole, they were, if anything, rising rather than falling from the early 1950s forward. Since the mid-1970s, and especially since the early 1990s, fertility rates in the poorest countries have all fallen, some more dramatically than others. The most substantial declines were in Asia, notably Vietnam, Myanmar, India, Nepal, and Uzbekistan. Nevertheless, they remain high, with a group of

Figure 2.3
Total Fertility Rate Trends by Country—Lower-Income Countries

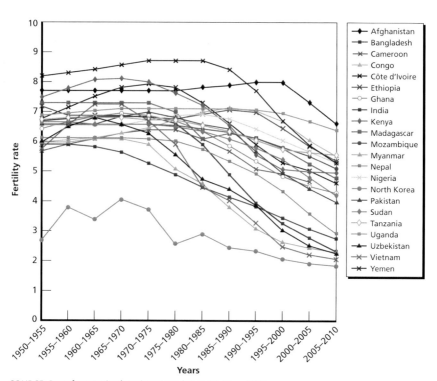

SOURCE: Data from United Nations Population Division, 2009.
RAND *MG1091-2.3*

14 countries exhibiting fertility rates clustered between 4 and 5.5 children per female. In general, the world's poor countries are roughly 20 years behind its middle-income countries in terms of their demographic transition to lower fertility rates.

Finally, Figure 2.4 spotlights the 14 largest countries of Latin America, the region from which the United States draws the major share of its immigrants. The pattern of falling fertility rates recurs but from much higher starting points. Cuba's fertility rates are similar to those of Western Europe. Guatemala, a poor country, still has very high fertility rates, followed closely by rates in Haiti, a poorer one. Fertility rates in the other countries, however, have, in recent years, fallen toward ZPG within a fairly narrow range, from a TFR just under

Figure 2.4
Total Fertility Rate Trends by Country—Latin America

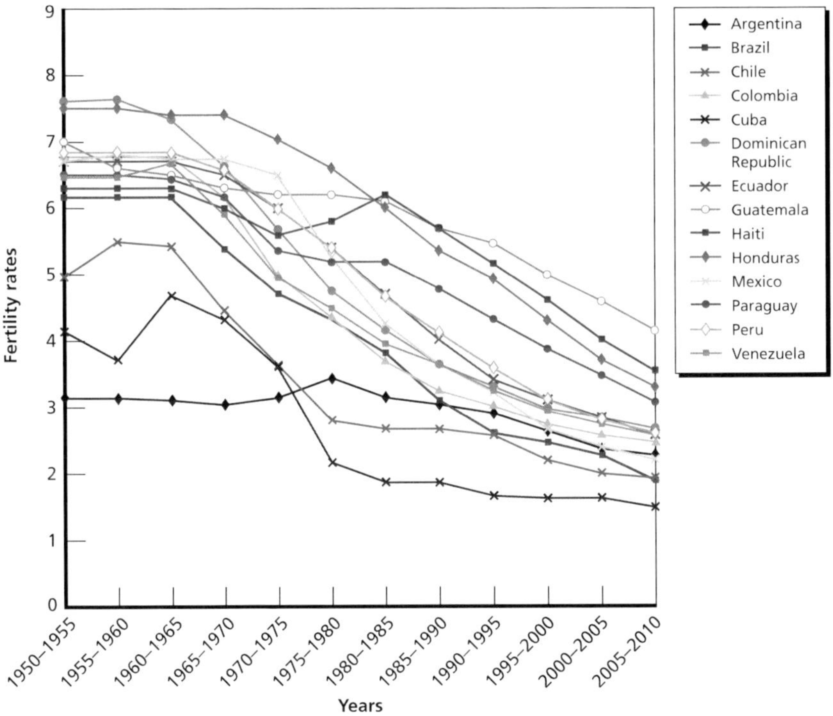

SOURCE: Data from United Nations Population Division, 2009.
RAND *MG1091-2.4*

2.0 (Chile and Brazil) to 3.5 (Honduras). The former notion of Latin America as teeming with babies is outdated. Latin American fertility rates as a whole may well hit ZPG between 2015 and 2020.

The fall in birthrates can also be inferred by asking in which years the country's largest (surviving) cohort was born. Figure 2.5 depicts these years.[8] China's largest cohort, for instance, consists of the population that was born between 1968 and 1973—people who are now in

---

[8]   The statistics from this chart were taken from the U.S. Census Bureau, *International Data Base (IDB)*, as of September 30, 2009. The reason for departing from the U.S. data is to generate an estimate for 2008 based on cohorts whose age end-points were a multiple of 5 years. Since these are historical data, differences in projections methodologies do not come into play.

Figure 2.5
Birth Years of Country's Largest Five-Year Cohort

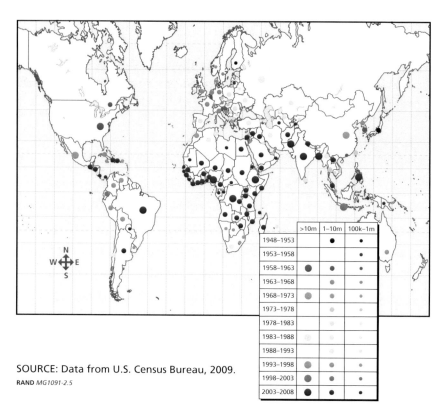

	>10m	1–10m	100k–1m
1948–1953		●	•
1953–1958			•
1958–1963	●	●	•
1963–1968		●	•
1968–1973	●	●	•
1973–1978		•	•
1978–1983			
1983–1988			
1988–1993			
1993–1998	●	●	•
1998–2003	●	●	•
2003–2008	●	●	•

SOURCE: Data from U.S. Census Bureau, 2009.
RAND *MG1091-2.5*

their late 30s and early 40s. Every subsequent cohort has been smaller. Even with the United States, which (currently) has a ZPG fertility rate and high levels of net immigration, the largest cohort consists of people born between 1958 and 1963, a group now in their late 40s and early 50s (although if the number of births in 2007—an all-time record— characterizes the next few years, such a graph, drawn five years hence, would show that its most recent cohort is the largest). Nearly 45 percent of all people live in countries whose most recent cohort is their largest—clear indication that their populations are still going up. However, the other 55 percent have, so far, already seen their largest cohort, and many of them may never again see a larger cohort.

Figure 2.6 characterizes all countries by their current total fertility rates.[9] Note that the legend for both this and the previous figure refers to the size of each country's peak cohort—countries with larger cohorts are denoted by larger circles.

Finally, to make the same point using global statistics, Table 2.1 shows the world's distribution of population by age and sex.[10] Note the inflection point (or deceleration) in the data that occurs in the early 20s

Figure 2.6
Current Total Fertility Rate by Country

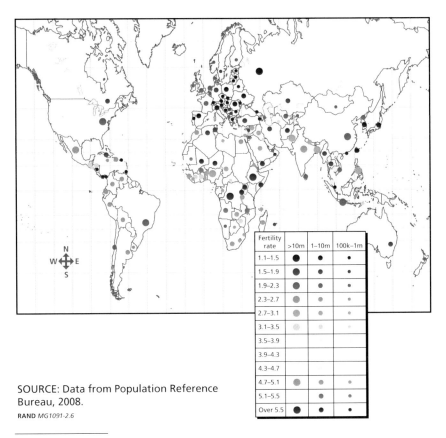

SOURCE: Data from Population Reference
Bureau, 2008.
RAND MG1091-2.6

---

[9]   These data were taken from the Population Reference Bureau, "2008 World Population Data Sheet," Washington, D.C., 2008. The reason for using this source was to get data for 2008. United Nations (UN) data, by contrast, give an estimate/projection for the 2005–2010 interval.

[10]   U.S. Census Bureau, 2009.

Table 2.1
Global Age Distribution, 2010
(in millions)

Age	Male	Female	Ratio
0–4	331.7	310.0	1.07
5–9	318.7	297.0	1.07
10–14	312.4	291.7	1.07
15–19	314.4	294.7	1.07
20–24	312.3	296.7	1.05
25–29	282.7	272.2	1.04
30–34	255.8	247.7	1.03
35–39	247.6	241.1	1.03
40–44	231.1	226.8	1.02
45–49	204.4	203.0	1.01
50–54	174.3	175.5	0.99
55–59	151.8	156.0	0.97
60–64	114.5	121.1	0.95
65–69	83.3	92.0	0.91
70–74	65.0	77.4	0.84
75–79	43.6	56.5	0.77
80–84	24.9	37.4	0.67
85–89	10.6	19.5	0.54
90–94	3.1	6.9	0.44
95–99	0.7	2.1	0.32
100+	0.1	0.4	0.24

SOURCE: U.S. Census Bureau, 2009.

Figure 2.7
Expected Changes in Working-Age Populations, 2010–2030

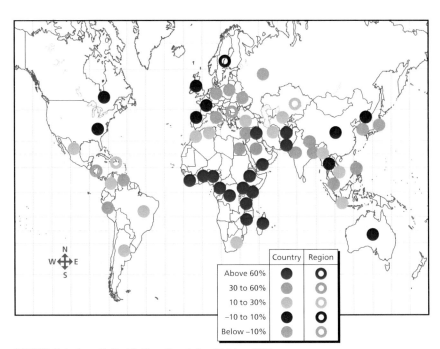

SOURCE: Data from United Nations Population Division, 2009.
RAND *MG1091-2.7*

- a northern swath that includes the United States, Canada, Britain,
  France, and Scandinavia, which tends to be immigrant-tolerant
  and whose cohorts should remain steady or rise slowly throughout
  the period
- middle-income countries (China, South Korea, Southeast Asia,
  Iran, Turkey, and the Maghreb) that will see modest increases
  in their working-age populations, but with noticeable inflection
  points (or in the case of East Asia, deflection points) circa 2025
- Latin America and Central America, whose population statistics
  will show similar patterns—growth followed by inflection circa
  2025—with the latter growing somewhat faster
- a South Asian swath, including the Ganges and Indus river val-
  leys, where population growth is steady at 2 percent a year (decel-

erating to 1 percent a year after 2030 if global fertility rates converge). Note that this does not include the southern third of India, which is demographically similar to Southeast Asia.

- two regions—sub-Saharan Africa and the core Arab states— that will continue to see vigorous growth in their working-age populations.

These generalizations are quite robust over the plausible variations in fertility rates. The difference between two very different fertility rate projections turns out to be quite modest, even 40 years out. Figure 2.8 illustrates as much by charting the trajectory of working-age populations from the 15 largest countries under both the medium-fertility and constant-fertility variants. Many of the line pairs look like one (e.g., China's); others show slight differences as one gets beyond 2030.[39]

The closeness of the constant-fertility and medium-fertility lines suggests that the projections of working-age populations by country by 2050 can be considered fairly solid, regardless of plausible variations in fertility rates, as long as the basic factors underlying migration— notably the search for economic opportunity and national variations in the acceptability of immigrants—do not change much. These numbers cannot be wished away on the theory that the world may turn out differently because there is very wiggle little room in these numbers.

Figures 2.9 and 2.10 look at the relative sizes of working-age populations in two theaters strategic to the United States: first the Atlantic and then the Pacific.

A few quick observations follow. Total working-age populations are shrinking, but the U.S. (and for a while, Turkish) working-age populations are growing. Cohorts in the United Kingdom and

---

[39] Why are the lines so close together even 40 years out? First, the difference between birthrates in both models takes time to emerge fully; after all, fertility rates do not jump up or down radically from one year to the next. Second, the graphs measure those over 20 and thus reflect only births that take place by 2030; therefore, differences in birthrates after that date do not matter. Third, demographic projections have a built-in momentum: Many countries with low (or, conversely, high) fertility rates in prior decades will have female cohorts of childbearing age whose ranks are low (or, conversely, high) relative to the population as a whole; thus, the number of children they would have would be correspondingly reduced.

Figure 2.8
Projected Populations for 15 Large Countries: Medium Variant and
Constant-Fertility Variant Forecasts Compared

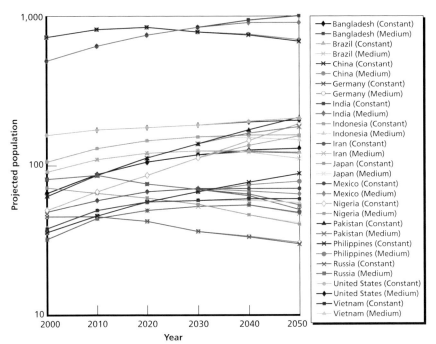

SOURCE: Data from United Nations Population Division, 2009.
RAND MG1091-2.8

France remain constant. Thus, the cohorts generated by everyone else are shrinking even faster than the overall totals. In 2008, everyone else's cohorts outnumbered U.S. cohorts by a ratio of 1.9 to 1 (without Turkey: 1.65). By 2050, this ratio should shrink to just over 1.4 to 1 (without Turkey: 1.15). Although such numbers suggest that Europe's ability to generate military power is not keeping up, the key question is: keeping up with whom? If the answer is Russia, for instance, note that the ratio of working-age populations between the North Atlantic Treaty Organization (NATO) and Russia rises from 5.9 today to 8.9 in 2050 (medium projection).

Demographically, the United States plays a smaller role in the Pacific, and China, of course, plays the larger role; it accounts for

Figure 2.9
Working-Age Populations for NATO Countries (in millions)

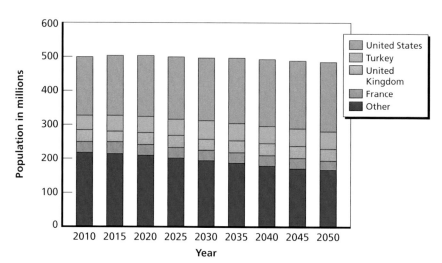

SOURCE: Data from United Nations Population Division, 2009.
RAND MG1091-2.9

roughly 58 percent of the total working-age population. By 2050, China's share will have shrunk to 51 percent (in the medium variant; 49.5 percent for the constant-fertility variant). The U.S. share is expected to stay relatively constant at 12 percent through 2025, whereupon it jumps to 15 percent by 2050. The traditional affluent U.S. allies in the region—e.g., South Korea, Taiwan, Japan—are facing declining working-age populations: Their share is expected to fall from nearly 9 to closer to 6 percent. The difference is made up by Southeast Asia, notably the Philippines, but also Indonesia to some extent.

Youth Bulges to Come?

Concerns have been expressed that, "Over the next few decades . . . dramatic demographic trends in developing nations . . . [such as] resur-

Figure 2.10
Working-Age Populations for Asia-Pacific Countries (in millions)

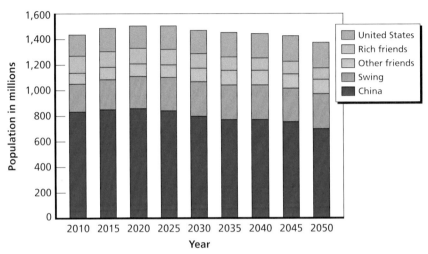

SOURCE: Data from United Nations Population Division, 2009.
NOTES: China includes Hong Kong and Macao and adds North Korea. The swing states are Brunei,
Cambodia, Indonesia, Laos, Myanmar, Papua New Guinea, and Vietnam. Other friends are
Thailand and the Philippines. The rich friends are Australia, Japan, New Zealand, South Korea,
Singapore, and Taiwan.
RAND *MG1091-2.10*

gent youth booms in the Muslim world . . . will give rise to dangerous
new security threats."[40]

Figures 2.11 and 2.12 examine the prospects by charting the percentage of the total population consisting of males between the ages
of 15 and 25 for the 45 middle- and lower-income countries included
in Figures 2.2 and 2.3. Figure 2.12 charts Islamic-majority countries;
Figure 2.11 charts the rest. Numbers for 2000 and 2005 are estimated;
those for 2010 and forward are projected. Those prior to 2025 are solid,
to the extent that these youths have already been born. Numbers for
2030 and beyond depend, to some extent, on future fluctuations in
fertility rates (the graphs use the medium-fertility variant). As the figures illustrate, any youth bulge is likely to be small and, in most cases,

[40] Neil Howe and Richard Jackson, "Battle of the (Youth) Bulge," *The National Interest*,
July/August 2008, pp. 33–40.

Figure 2.11
Percentage of Population Composed of Males Aged 15 to 25—Non–Islamic-Majority Countries

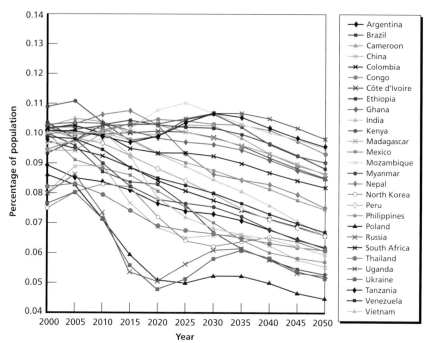

SOURCE: Data from United Nations Population Division, 2009.
RAND *MG1091-2.11*

negative: The percentage of the population composed of young men is likely to shrink rather than grow.

Projected Muslim Populations

The world's Islamic population tends to be geographically concentrated. Although Muslims account for 23 percent of the world's population, up to 69 percent of the world's Islamic population lives in countries that are more than 87 percent Islamic. This means that the size of the Islamic population is closely tied to the size of predominantly Islamic states, thereby limiting the impact of uncertainties over whether Islamic populations within countries have been counted cor-

Figure 2.12
Percentage of Population Composed of Males Aged 15 to 25—Islamic-Majority Countries

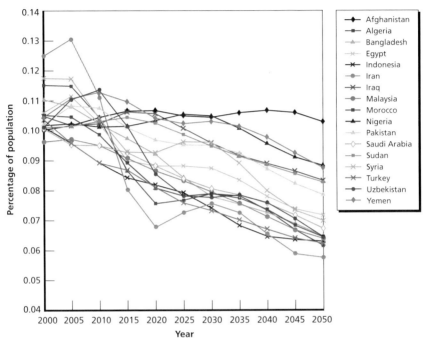

SOURCE: Data from United Nations Population Division, 2009.
RAND MG1091-2.12

rectly. Many other Muslims live in countries in which their populations are geographically concentrated—e.g., the northern half of Nigeria and the northern two-thirds of Sudan. Of the 21 percent of the world's Islamic population that does not live in Islamic-majority countries, almost half live in India.

Because Islamic-majority countries tend to have high fertility rates (although not all do—e.g., Iran), their populations tend to be young. The percentage of the world's working-age populations who are Islamic is, thus, at 24.4 percent in 2010, somewhat lower than its share of the overall population (25.6 percent). By 2030, the percentage is expected to be 28.2 percent and by 2050, 30.7 percent.[41]

Considerable attention is given to the Eurabia question:[42] What share of Europe will be Muslim? One problem is that estimates of today's Muslim population are, in many countries, only that: estimates. Neither France nor the United States allows their national census to ask such a question. Estimates of age distributions or fertility rates are on an even less firm basis. Nevertheless, one can make an attempt at an estimate that is contingent on several assumptions.[43]

Consider France, whose Muslim population has been estimated at 8.5 percent of the national total. Assume that, because Algeria has been the most important source of Muslim immigrants in the post–World War II period, the Islamic population's fertility rate and age distribution are the same as Algeria's today,[44] but with survival rates the same as France as a whole. Assume further that two-thirds of all

---

[41] This assumes medium-variant projections; the percentage is 31.6 percent under constant-fertility projections.

[42] This attention is ironic, however, because only a small percentage of the world's Muslim population resides in Europe or is expected to, even by 2050. The term *Eurabia* was popularized by Niall Ferguson's "The Way We Live Now: Eurabia?" *New York Times Sunday Magazine*, April 4, 2004. See also Christopher Caldwell, *Reflections on the Revolution in Europe: Immigration, Islam, and the West*, New York: Doubleday, 2009.

[43] In making our projections, we have to assume several things that make sense only in aggregate. First, the offspring of Islamic parents are Islamic (statistically speaking, one has to assume something similarly proportional from mixed marriages). Second, Islam as a category is nominal and binary (one is or one is not Muslim—religiosity is not a variable). Third, the net "migration" (conversion) into and out of Islam is zero, or at least statistically negligible, everywhere. We begin our analysis with a fourth assumption that the age distribution, fertility rate, and death rate of the Islamic population in any country are the same as the non-Islamic population of the country (there have been countries in which the percent of the population that is Islamic has grown for reasons having little to do with migration—e.g., Lebanon and Serbia/Yugoslavia). Later, we explore alternative assumptions for each country.

[44] Although NRC, 2000, p. 173, observes that ". . . migrants have fertility levels in between those of their countries of origin and destination," Charles F. Westoff and Tomas Frejka, "Religiousness and Fertility Among European Muslims," *Population and Development Review*, Vol. 33, No. 4, 2007, pp. 785–809, suggests that Muslim birthrates, while still higher than native European ones, are on par with birthrates that prevail in the countries from which they came.

Figure 3.1
Gross National Product per Working-Age Person Relative to U.S. Levels
(logarithmic scale)

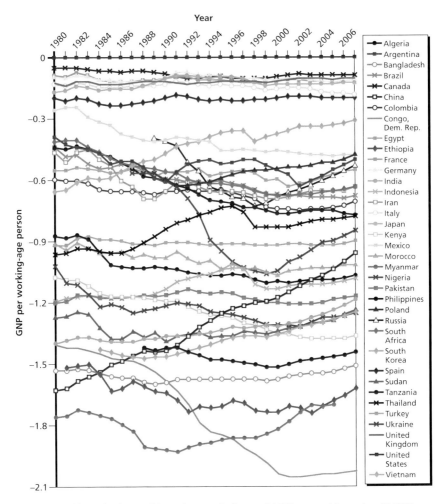

SOURCE: World Databank, "World Development Indicators, 2007," accessed December 15, 2010.
RAND *MG1091-3.1*

mean that a nation's GDP per capita is growing faster than the U.S.
rate. Declining lines mean that it is growing more slowly, although it
could still be rising in absolute terms. Note that, for clarity, the figure

shows the logarithm of the ratio rather than the ratio itself; thus, the U.S. line equals zero (the natural logarithm of one).

What is notable about this graph is the stability of the various per capita GDPs vis-à-vis each other over such a long period.[9] Consider, first, six rich countries: Japan, Germany, France, the United Kingdom, Italy, and Spain. All of them (other than Spain) start roughly a quarter less affluent than the United States, and all of them (now including Spain) end up there as well. Indeed, Japan, whose per capita GDP reached 85 percent in the 1980s, is now closer to 75 percent. Canada stays in the 80- to 90-percent range throughout. Following several decades of economic convergence after World War II ended, there has been little further convergence since 1980 in these numbers.[10] If past is prologue, there is no reason to believe that these ratios will change much over the next 40 years.

After the rich countries comes a fairly large gap around the −0.5 level (roughly a third of U.S. GDP per capita). The gap is crossed by three countries: Mexico (whose income circa 1980 reflected the elevated price of crude oil and thus fell with crude oil prices in the early 1980s), Russia (whose GDP collapsed in the first five years after Communism ended), and South Korea—the only country that has moved from the middle-income band to the affluent band (albeit at the bottom of the band) over the last quarter-century.

Next examine the middle-income countries whose 2007 GDP per capita on the graph lies between −0.45 (36 percent of U.S. levels) and −0.85 (12 percent of U.S. levels). They include, from most to least affluent, Poland, Mexico, Argentina, Russia, Turkey, South Africa, Iran, Brazil, Colombia, Thailand, Algeria, and Ukraine. The overlap between this group and the 1980 version of the middle-income group is high. South Korea left that group going up, and Thailand entered that

---

[9] Bear in mind that the display—in portrait rather than landscape form and with the legend on the side—exaggerates the vertical dimension.

[10] Per capita GDP in Singapore (not shown), having nearly reached U.S. levels just before the Asian financial crisis in 1998, did surpass U.S. levels in 2005 and is still rising. Hong Kong levels may also surpass U.S. levels within the next few years, based on recent trends. Data for Taiwan are unavailable. Incidentally, the impact of the 1998 financial crisis, as judged by the data, was quite substantial and persistent.

Figure 4.1
Number of Old-Old People (85+) for Every 100 Working-Age Adults

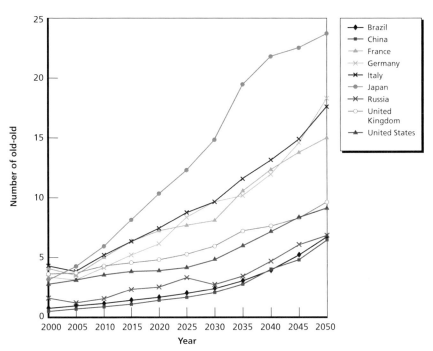

SOURCE: Data from United Nations Population Division, 2009.
RAND MG1091-4.1

Reintroducing the earlier basis of comparison, China remains the country, among those assessed, with the lowest proportion of old-old relative to potential workers, while Japan clearly has the greatest. The proportions for France, Germany, Italy, and the United Kingdom also rise to the double digits, but those for Brazil, Russia, and the United States stay below 10. We now explore these figures in more detail to explore the extent to which demographic changes affect national power. Countries that are similar today may face very different futures, particularly if they have no good way other than taxation to support those who cannot work but who, on average, face high health care requirements.

The Advanced Countries

As noted, our projections for the older population encompass France, Germany, Italy, Japan, the United Kingdom, and the United States. These are among the richest countries in the world and together constituted 53 percent of the world economy in 2007, when measured at market exchange rates.[8] The fact that they have populations that are older than those of many other countries, at least in the case of the first four, can be credited to lower total fertility ratios among women of childbearing age and higher survival rates among older residents. The United States and the United Kingdom have slower-aging populations than the other four. In the case of the United States, its fertility rate is the highest of the six, while its survival rates (the number of people of a given age who survive until the next year as a percentage of all people of a given age) for those older than age 60 are relatively low. For the United Kingdom, even though its fertility rate is closer to the average for the entire group, it has lower survival rates for most age groups above age 70.

Chapter One discussed variations in total fertility rates and how those might change. This section takes an alternative look at how populations age by considering changes in survival rates. The possibility of such changes is not far-fetched. Humans have undergone astounding physical and longevity changes in the past 300 years.[9] These include an increase in average body size by more than 50 percent, more than a doubling of average longevity, and improvements in "the robustness and capacity of vital organ systems."[10] Even beyond these longer-term changes in longevity, recent research suggests that longevity could be malleable even in the short term: Current conditions and behav-

---

[8]   World Databank, 2010.

[9]   Robert W. Fogel and Dora L. Costa, "A Theory of Technophysio Evolution, with Some Implications for Forecasting Population, Health Care Costs, and Pension Costs," *Demography*, Vol. 34, No. 1, February 1997, pp. 49–66.

[10]   Fogel and Costa, 1997, p. 49.

Trade-Offs Between Fertility Rates and Migration Rates

The prospect of a nation losing power in the long run by failing to produce enough babies may press governments to find ways to raise population levels. In essence, there are three ways to do so: raise birth-rates, increase migration, or lower death rates. The last, lowering death rates, may be virtuous for its own sake, but with death rates among those under 60 as low as they are, there is not much, demographically, to be gained by improving them. This leaves a choice, essentially, between babies and newcomers.[1] To test the trade-off, we will start with German numbers as a test case. Germany now has a nearly 40-year history of below-replacement fertility rates and modest but positive immigration levels. The largest cohorts are in their early middle ages: For

---

[1]   Jonathan Grant, Stijn Hoorens, Suja Sivadasan, Mirjam van het Loo, Julie DaVanzo, Lauren Hale, Shawna Gibson, and William Butz, *Low Fertility and Population Ageing: Causes, Consequences, and Policy Options*, Santa Monica, Calif.: RAND Corporation, MG-206-EC, 2004, p. 24, notes:

> The effectiveness of migration as a strategy towards preventing population ageing and a decrease in the size of the population depends on the ability of national governments to implement suitable migration policies. . . . The extent to which immigrants are ready and able to integrate into the receiving population appears to be a crucial factor for the success of immigration strategies [often discussed] . . . in terms of the 'quality' of the population, a term used in a similar context as social cohesion [and covering what] portion of immigrants [come] with low educational attainment. . . . In order to avoid such a development towards social exclusion, it has been argued that Western Europe would be better served by relatively small contingents of immigrants and a partial recovery of native fertility, than by continued extremely low native fertility that is offset by a very large immigration stream.

every two-year-old, there are two 42-year-olds. The total fertility rate is 1.41, which, if not supplemented by migration, ultimately implies a demographic half-life of just under two generations. Germany, however, has (or recently had) a net immigration rate of two per year per thousand—slightly less than half of U.S. levels.

Demographically, this country's future is fairly grim. Figure B.1 shows the population of adults ages 20 through 60 (i.e., working age) over time, assuming a constant fertility rate and a net immigration rate. The current parameters result in a workforce that shrinks from 45 million in 2008 to 24 million in 2100. If immigration is stopped or dries up, the fall is greater—to 15 million. Comparing the two numbers suggests that by 2100, only 60 percent of the working-age population will be descendents of those who were residents in 2008. Note that

Figure B.1
Working-Age Population Projection of a Hypothetical Germany-Like Country with Alternative Birth and Migration Rates

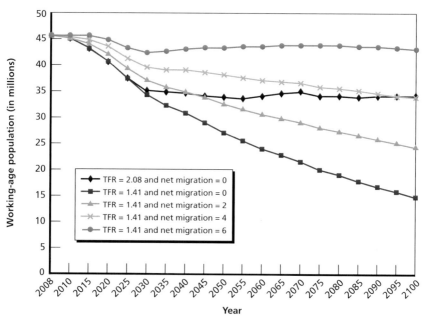

SOURCE: Generated by a model based on data from United Nations Population Division, 2009.
RAND MG1091-B.1

the underlying trends are only somewhat ameliorated if the fertility rate were to return to 2.08 (which generates ZPG in countries with low mortality rates). Absent migration, the working-age population drops to 34 million in 2035 before leveling (because babies not born earlier mean fewer childbearing women later).

Can migration make up the difference? Because the average age of migrants into affluent nations is in the low twenties, most immigrants add to the labor force on arrival; babies, not for 20 years or so. In Figure B.1, one gets to the same workforce by 2100 with the current (1.41) fertility rate and four immigrants per thousand as one does with a ZPG fertility rate. The demographic payoff from more rapid migration comes earlier, but after 2100 the higher fertility rate produces some higher numbers. Finally, if the migration rate hits six per thousand, the size of the workforce hardly declines over the following century. Admittedly, a migration rate of six per thousand is three times Germany's current rate, but it is only somewhat higher than the U.S. rate (five per thousand) and lower than Canada's (seven per thousand).

For comparison purposes, let us take another type of country, one which has had a ZPG fertility rate (2.08) for as far back as anyone can remember but which faces the immediate prospect that the fertility rate will fall to 1.7. What immigration rates should it seek if its goal is to preserve the size of the workforce? Figure B.2 illustrates some trade-offs.

The bottom line shows the base case: The workforce stays constant until the newborns enter the labor force and then starts to drop once more people leave than enter the workforce. By 2100, the workforce is down to 30 million and dropping. A migration rate of two to three per thousand can maintain the size of the workforce circa 2100, and in both cases the workforce rises somewhat in the first few decades, because migrants enter the workforce before newborns do. If the country wants to ensure that its workforce can achieve a steady state after 2100, it needs to attract (and retain) four migrants per year per thousand. Regardless of its migration rate, however, with a total fertility

Figure B.2
Working-Age Population Projection of a Hypothetical Country with ZPG Fertility Rates Under Alternative Future Fertility Rate and Migration Assumptions

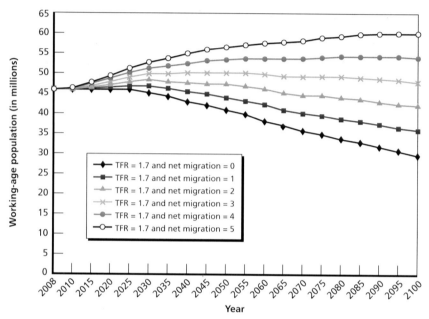

SOURCE: Generated by a model based on data from United Nations Population Division, 2009.
RAND *MG1091-B.2*

rate of 1.7, the size of the workforce that has descended from today's workforce will decline to 30 million.[2]

So, if the policy goal is to maintain the size of the workforce, then migration can be a substitute for births, at least over a period as long as a century. North American–level immigration rates can compensate for Germany-level fertility rates (going back to the early 1970s). European-level immigration rates can compensate for a decline of fertility rates to slightly higher levels that characterize England or Scandi-

---

[2]   Or less. The 30 million figure assumes that there is no emigration. If annual net immigration of, say, three per thousand is a combination of five immigrants per thousand and two emigrants per thousand, then the 30 million figure would be lower: 18 million (assuming that no immigrant was a descendent of a former emigrant).